FULLY INVOLVED

A GUIDE TO BEING IN A RELATIONSHIP WITH A FIREFIGHTER

BY MYNDA OHS, PHD

CONTENTS

CHAPTER SEVEN:
Talk Isn't Cheap Unless You Make It that Way
EPILOGUE:
Good to Go

<u>APPENDIX:</u>

Communication Activity Forms

DEDICATION

For Jeff, Megan, and Kyle.

I couldn't do it without you by my side.

Nor would I want to.

ACKNOWLEDGMENTS

I feel honored as a member of the Long Beach, California, fire family for over twenty years. The department members have impacted my life in more ways than I could count, both good and bad, but I wouldn't change a thing. I want to thank all the fire departments that have allowed me to be there for them and their families during some of the worst times they had to go through. I respect their struggles, their triumphs, and, always, their bravery. And, finally, my gratitude to my husband and children. When I started the book, I was the sole author, but when I would ask for Jeff's opinion on anything, his firefighter point of view was so insightful that I was thrilled that he offered to contribute. The same for my kids and their written contributions. All three are my co-authors, and, for doing such a brilliant job, I thank them.

INTRODUCTION
What I Do and Why

LIFE CHANGES WHEN YOU GET INVOLVED with a firefighter. I should know. I learned the hard way.

You would think I might have suspected how it would be. After all, I was an EMT for a private ambulance and worked with first responders every day when I met this guy who ended up being *the* guy, the one I would marry.

It's not like I was a stranger to difficult times or trauma. I was divorced and had a four-year-old daughter. I had been working as an EMT for three years. I'd seen a lot of situations I never could have prepared for. I learned later that these images would change me and be stuck in my memory forever.

Jeff and I met in the least romantic way possible—on a 911 call. I was the EMT, and he was the paramedic for the fire department. As an EMT, I was allowed to provide basic life support services, such as taking and recording vitals or splinting fractures. Only a paramedic could administer meds, start IVs, read EKGs, intubate people, and in other ways provide what are known as advanced life services. This meant that anytime I was out on a call, paramedics would be on the spot, too.

The day I met Jeff was on a call that my partner and I were dispatched to. We headed to a park for a person who was down for unknown reasons. On our way to the call, my partner told me there was a paramedic with the fire department that could be a jerk. I should just ignore him. As we arrived on scene, and I jumped out of the ambulance and walked to where everyone was standing, I was nervously looking around for this "guy" who was supposed to be a jerk.

When it turned out there was no need for an EMT on the spot, I headed back to where I'd come from. There had been several guys over there—I had no idea which one my partner had singled out. After we got back into the ambulance, I asked him, "So which guy is the jerk?"

Yes, you got it! The "jerk" turned out to be my husband-to-be. Without thinking, I said, "I think he's kind of cute."

My partner replied, *"Don't even think about it."*

That's how it started. We didn't rush into anything. Jeff and I would run into each other on calls, simply because we both happened to have been dispatched to the same place. We started talking more and more. Having a shared bond from running calls together, we grew closer.

I could understand why my partner had warned me off Jeff, even though I had already decided he was mistaken. Jeff wasn't a jerk. He was, however, pretty intense. He was passionate about what he did, and that was one of the things I ended up falling in love with. He cared for every single patient. Some medics get complacent and even jaded, not always treating the patients very kindly. Jeff cared, whether the patient was critically injured, seriously ill, or more or less a false alarm, someone who turned out not to have needed a paramedic at all.

It wasn't until we'd been running into each other on calls for a year that, on yet another call, Jeff asked me out. Not for a romantic candlelit dinner, but for a casual sushi lunch. I had a divorce behind me, and he was going through one. Still, it wasn't just another lunch with a teammate. Even as I drove away, I thought, *I'm going to marry that man.* And, after two years of living together, I did exactly that. And here we are, still together after twenty-one years of marriage.

I was living in Redlands, California, when we met, and Jeff was in San Bernardino. Not long after that lunch date, I moved into his San Bernardino house. Life was good. We were in love, finding the second time around sweeter, and we soon had a son, Kyle, to join my daughter Megan. I became a stay-at-home mom dealing with two small children. And then, when my daughter was seven and our son under a year old, everything changed. I got a crash course in discovering just how challenging it was to be a firefighter's spouse, all because Jeff decided he was going to follow his dream of working for Long Beach City Fire Department.

This wasn't just a little career change. It meant starting all over again, first at the academy and then as a rookie. In my mind, I was like, *Heck, yeah, follow your dreams.* I thought I had it handled, right? If you're a firefighter partner and reading this, you're probably laughing, knowing that Jeff might be following his dream but I was— temporarily, at least—living in a dream world.

Fire academy isn't hanging out with the guys having a lot of laughs the way it is in the movies. It's sixteen grueling weeks, from six a.m. to six p.m., and that's not counting tests and drills. To stay in, a student has to get above a 75 percent grade on every exam. A single grade of under 75 percent is allowed; the second time, it's all over. I discovered that academy students called classmates their "littermates" for good reason: Jeff spent more time with them than he did with me.

Not only was he working long hours, he was no longer working for the state of California or based in Yucaipa, about a fifteen-minute drive from our place. He was now studying to be a firefighter in Long Beach. That meant that in addition to being at the academy for so many hours, he had to commute from San Bernardino, a seventy-two-mile drive that takes an hour and a half at the best of times. I'd spend all day corralling two small children and cleaning up their spills and scuff marks, then my husband would come home—and often go straight to bed because he had to get up at 4:30 a.m. to head for the freeway. Years later, he still rises before dawn. "Sleeping in" for him means waking up at six.

Once Jeff graduated from the academy, he started working regular shifts as a rookie. The only difference from being a regular firefighter is that being a rookie involves "rites of passage." They're not exactly hazing, but they're not living the good life, either. Rookies are assigned to do all the chores, aren't allowed to watch television in the firehouse, must never be out of uniform, and get scheduled for loads of drills and trainings, geared to prove they can do the job. That's for a full year. Only the strong survive, and Jeff was damned if he wouldn't always be one of the strong ones.

If that sounds rough, well, it was. Not surprisingly, some marriages don't survive it. Ours almost didn't. We had a lot of stress in those early years. We fought a lot because I felt like I was stuck with the kids and couldn't have an enjoyable grown-up evening when my husband finally got home, because at that point his idea of an enjoyable grown-up evening was being sound asleep.

My life felt so dead-ended, I decided I had to get out of the house, if for no other reason than to sit on a toilet in peace without a child lying on the floor outside the door with his fingers waggling under it, and his lips pushed beneath as far as they'd go, while he called, "Mommy, Mommy, can you see my fingers?"

What I could see more than his fingers was that this would be one of those days when I'd want to rip my hair out, topped off by my husband coming home after a twenty-four-hour shift I knew had been a rough one for him, because I'd heard him speaking in *that* voice during our morning call, which meant he'd get home tired and cranky and living up to the nickname we had for him (and, yes, he knows about this), the Funsucker.

All that led me to school, which I loved. School became my thing for a few years. I got my bachelor's degree, which had been my original plan. Then, in 2000, I got my first master's degree, in school counseling. I considered being a school counselor, until the time came to work as a substitute teacher. *No way!* Whatever it took to deal with other people's sometimes spoiled, often bratty, always recalcitrant kids, I didn't have it. God bless those that teach! I had my own kids to drive me crazy, thank you very much. Instead, I worked for five years at an inpatient hospital specializing in children and adolescents. Working with kids was rewarding, and it's still one of my favorite things to do.

I went back to school to get another master's, in marriage and family therapy, which I completed in 2005, in order to qualify for a state license to start my own practice. I worked with families and children through the court system. During that time, I also began teaching in different areas—anger management and suicide prevention are two—and doing couples workshops.

That's when I really got the bug for teaching and decided to get my PhD in 2008. Like I said, I *loved* school. It was during that journey to my doctorate that I decided I wanted to get back to working with first responders.

In the back of my mind, I had known for quite a while that this was what I wanted, ever since my own experiences as an EMT. I remember having a call for a little girl who was having seizures we couldn't stop. She was about the same age as my daughter, so it hit home, and hard. I dropped her off at the ER and walked to the ambulance to clean it up. To my surprise, when I got there, I started crying and couldn't stop. After I got home the next morning, I just lay in bed with my daughter and worried about the other child for days. I was with EMS for roughly four years, so I logged many similar calls that still affect me to this day. I remember them and tears come to my eyes, or my stomach turns over.

In those days, it wasn't even okay to talk about it. As a woman in a field dominated by men, I couldn't risk being seen as weak or unable to handle the job. I had to hide it and pretend it didn't bother me.

But it does bother all first responders at some point. It's not *if* being a first responder will affect you, but *when*. I wanted to give others the counseling I hadn't received.

With my doctorate, I found a job working on a marine base in Twentynine Palms, California, doing suicide prevention and education. I stayed for a year and a half, and during that time found the company I now work for, which works only with first responders. I started in 2014 and realized it was what I wanted to do for the rest of my life. My first year was the hardest ever—running eleven line of duty deaths with various fire and police departments—but it made me sure I was where I was supposed to be.

Jeff was supportive when I first went back to school, but as I became more involved in my studies, my career also became a cause for resentment and jealousy. A competition began for who had it hardest. It was a no-win situation for me, because I would feel guilty after any fight and blame myself for not rising above it all.

If you're a firefighter spouse, I'm sure you know how tiring these battles are. There was no counseling for fire families then that I knew of, and even if it had been available, it wouldn't have occurred to me to seek help. I was too certain that it was all my fault, that I was a bad wife. Why would I want to share my failure with others?

My own problems and busy schedule as the wife of a firefighter and mother of two kids nagged at me, but I was helping children and families and then first responders, which made up for all the other stuff. Now I can't imagine doing anything else. I still work with not just firefighters and cops but also those in other stressful, high-PTSD jobs, such as air marshals, and both corrections and probation officers. In an average month, that may include traditional talk therapy, speaking at conferences, teaching at fire or police departments on different topics, leading workshops for firefighters and their significant others, and doing Critical Incident Stress Management (CISM) for officer-related, in-custody deaths, line of duty deaths (LODD), and critical calls that may affect a fire crew or police officers. CISM is designed to help the people working at the site or in the department where a critical incident has taken place, to give them the opportunity to process the incident before they even leave work, in order to prevent the start of PTSD.

I am also trained in EMDR, which is Eye Movement Desensitization Reprocessing, a technique using eye movement to reprogram and replicate rapid eye movement (REM) such as we experience at the deepest level of sleep. The extensive training and supervision teaches counselors how to "unstick" the traumatic memories that get imprinted in the mind of someone when they've seen too much horror.

And all this brings us to you, and why I have written this book.

I found it challenging to be the significant other of a firefighter. I realized that if I—a psychologist and former EMT—had trouble with this feat and its truckload of adjustments, it must be even harder for others—men and women, spouses and parents, and children as well. As someone who talks to firefighters all the time, more than I talk to anyone else, I *know* they reveal things to me they don't share with the people who love them. I know how they feel and think. I also know how much they don't tell their life partners, and how unaware they often are as to how those partners might feel.

There are almost 30,000 fire departments in the United States, with more than a million career and volunteer firefighters. That makes for a lot of significant others. I don't think anyone else can address those significant others—others like you—quite like I can, from my perspective as a spouse and a counselor, on a professional as well as a brutally honest personal level.

I'm thankful my marriage survived the fire family lifestyle. Many relationships don't. I had to learn by trial and error. Why should you? I want significant others to know that we all go through what you're going through. We all have the same fights about the same things. And with the right outlook and skills, your relationship, like mine, can survive this challenging life.

If this sounds serious and painful, I assure you that I bring to this a mixed bag and not a sack of woe. I hope you'll have some belly laughs, a few gasps of surprise, a tear or two when you think of your own memories or empathize with others' stories, and plenty of tales that will make you think.

Most important of all, I pledge to give you everything I can, all that I've learned, both as a Clinician and as a wife who loves her fantastic husband. You'll learn why being with your partner rarely resembles living with someone outside the fire world. I'll share with you the challenges and obstacles a firefighter faces, and how they shape the firefighter personality, often making life rough for those at home. Then we'll talk about the many things (you can't even imagine how many, if you're new at this!) that you may not have planned for, the realities of being married to the job—even if it's by one degree of separation. Trust me, we're all married to that job, if we love someone in it.

We'll look at the firefighter traits that can wreck homes and the unique challenges that come with the commitment to be that person's significant other, and, via chapters from my daughter and son, see what it's like to grow up in a firefighter family, how it affects everyone.

We'll work together to help you identify your personal challenges, and I'll assist you in owning your responsibility and discovering how to be more flexible. We'll work on the all-important skill of communication, which has to be done differently in a fire family, and we'll talk about how to recognize when you need special help and where to get it. Finally, I'll talk about the difficult issues of retirement, emergencies, and line of duty deaths, and how and why you need to be prepared for all eventualities in order to get on with your lives.

It matters to me that at the end you close this book armed with no-nonsense advice on how to cope, grow, and flourish in your relationship—and how to make that relationship one in which you're a full partner in your firefighter's life, the two of you working in tandem to have a shared life that has ups and down like all others, but is based on mutual respect and pride in saving the homes, livelihoods, and lives of others.

This book is to reassure you, cheer you on, and help you see how to adapt, how to take care of yourself, how to ask for more, and when to give more.

I have four messages for firefighters' partners who have wondered how they can do this—and if they even *want* to do it. These are the things I wish someone had told me back when I was struggling to bring up two young children, feeling consumed by loneliness much of the time, frustrated by a demanding or depressed mate when he was home, and wondering all too often if divorce was the only answer.

1. You're not alone. You are not a failure as a spouse, and you must not take it personally. You can start by stepping back and accepting that you are part of fire family culture now, and that things will get better. I want to help you by explaining what your partner doesn't tell you, what I've learned by being in a fire family, and what I've discovered from my special perspective as a psychologist counseling firefighters. I want you to know how they think and how it affects you.

2. Bring married/engaged/committed to the fire service is a unique circumstance that requires a unique set of skills. You need to fill your toolbox with new skills to cope. I see my job as being the supply sergeant who provides you with these.

3. You need to major in compromises. Each person wants the other to change. Each person thinks, "It's not my problem." That kind of thinking leads to behavior that's a serious red flag in any relationship: no longer working at communication, or using communication not as a tool to solve problems, but as a bat for beating the other person over the head. Compromise is the key. You give, you get.

4. A firefighter relationship works in the long run only when it is an equal partnership. As a firefighter's partner, you have signed up for something that might never be a day at the beach, but which will bring you happiness, love, and fulfilment. The key? Never forget that you're on the same team. Your mission is the same.

The title of this book says it all. In the fire world, "fully involved" refers to a building that is totally engulfed, flames pouring from the windows. In a relationship with a firefighter, you must be fully involved as well. Your partner is totally consumed by the fire world—because being a firefighter *is* all-consuming. It's not like being a CPA, mechanic, or marketing director. It's not even close to working a normal schedule.

That means that as a significant other, you can't help but be consumed as well. Your own home life and career have to take place in this other world. You have no choice but to be fully involved if you want your relationship to succeed. The challenge is to retain your identity as a partner, to be a real partner, and to be strong and not passive.

It can be done. You have not chosen the easiest life, but I'm here to assure you it will be a great one, as long as you're fully involved.

SECTION ONE

The Firefighter's World

CHAPTER ONE

You Didn't Fall for an Alien from Another Planet—
Just Someone from Another World

WHAT'S IT LIKE BEING A FIREFIGHTER, and why is it harder for firefighters, men and women, to be average Joes and Janes at home?

I know this question is one that someone in a relationship with a firefighter can't always answer. One reason is that firefighters are rarely the most communicative people at home, even though they communicate well at work. That's the weird thing about it. They must be able to communicate every little thing to each other, because their lives depend on knowing where everyone is and what everyone is doing at all times. Their career isn't like any other; neither their training nor their culture encourages them to share their feelings. It's a gift and a curse, really. It's a survival skill. They have to deal with the horrible things they see on a daily basis. Their behavior is the result of having to separate from their emotions to get the job done and handle an emergency. Unfortunately, this doesn't work at home with the people they love.

More importantly, at least until they've been in a relationship with a firefighter for a long time, most "normal" people—pretty much all of us who aren't firefighters—don't realize they're involved with someone from another world. That world is the Fire World. When you become part of a firefighter couple or a firefighter family, you're in that world, a stranger in a strange land.

It may feel uncomfortable at first, but think of it this way: if you were to go live in China, what would you be willing to do to fit in and feel a part of your new home? You would learn the language, religious beliefs, and cultural practices. You might go and visit popular tourist sites or make new friends.

This is the same attitude you need to adopt when you decide to be in a relationship with a firefighter.

Why did your partner decide to become a firefighter? Mine kind of fell into it. His family moved from the Bay Area to a small town in Northern California that relied heavily on volunteer firefighters. There was a large fire near his house, and he ended up helping out by doing many of the less glamorous things. But he was hooked—charged up and excited. Filthy and tired, he asked the chief if there was a way he could get more involved. He joined them as a "junior" firefighter, allowed to do only what was basically the dirty work and cleanup. His dad actually had to drive him to the scenes until he got his driver's license—and eventually got involved as well. By eighteen, Jeff was taking classes to start what would be his career.

The Three Facets of a Firefighter's Work World

The first step in surviving as a fire service significant other is to gain an objective perspective of what it's like to be a firefighter. Let's start by taking a look at the three facets of a firefighter's work world, because every workday will fall into one of these categories:

1. Routine day at the fire station
2. Busy call day
3. Fire season

Routine days at the fire station might be calm, as far as runs go, but that doesn't mean they aren't busy in their own way. Firefighters always have plenty to do; their work lives are largely planned out. And even though they're no longer tasked with all the chores that were handed to them when they were rookies (they have another set of rookies for those now), it's not about sitting around rehashing past calls or playing cards or video games.

All firefighters have specific stationhouse maintenance jobs, much like roommates do. They also have training and drills to follow and carry out, along with regular station inspections and the preparations for them.

Firefighting is a physically demanding job. Therefore, time is set aside every day for working out. If you think about how much time they are at work, it makes sense that they would need to work out at the station. This helps not only their physical well-being, but their mental health as well. I have heard many regular people make comments like, "Must be nice to get paid to work out." I doubt those people would be willing to put up with everything else that comes with it.

At the station, the crew interacts much as a family does—because this *is* a family, the "fire family." They joke and talk, are together constantly, and form strong bonds. They're still "littermates," just as they were at the academy, because they don't go home for days on end. The basic schedules (not including overtime days, which will add to these already long days) are:

- the 48/96— forty-eight hours on and ninety-six hours off
- the Kelly One, also known as the 4/4 or 4/6—a four-day set on and four or six days off
- the Kelly Two, or the 3/4—a three-day set on and four days off

Every schedule means the firefighter spends almost as much time at the station, day and night, as at home. This impacts the firefighter family as much as, if not even more than, the firefighter.

Seriously. When you're involved with a firefighter, you'll never be sympathetic to the complaints of nine-to-fivers or their partners again. I mean, they get to lead normal lives!

Even though a great deal of time is spent at the station on routine days, they still get called out; how much depends on how busy the station is. Especially at the busier stations—and there is always one that's the busiest—the crew has little downtime and rarely gets to sleep soundly through the night. Some people prefer the busy stations, love the pace, and don't like if they get detailed out to a quieter station temporarily to fill a gap. We also have what we call "retirement stations," popular with older firefighters, who prefer the slower pace.

If you're a significant other, you probably already know that stations have a captain who is in charge of the station. There are firefighter-paramedics, who are responsible for running medical aids as well as

cations to

that sit in

Finally, th

provide ar

My hu

ambulanc

there will

was an EM

patient; it'

carries thr

exception

cially quali

The er

out. Even on days with no calls or just an occa

a firefighter spends the day on edge, tense

ilance, which we'll come back to late

in bed, the firefighter is waiting i

of sleep. Don't get fooled if

Remember, it's not restful

I learned this les

the morning and

one question

of day w

slep

Above the captain, who is the head of one station, is the battalion chief, in charge of several stations. In a multi-station call, the captains are in charge until the battalion chief gets onboard.

Got all that?

It's important to know the organizational structure because it impacts the way firefighters think. They're in an environment with a paramilitary structure, with specific duties and strict rules for handling situations. This shapes their personalities, and they bring those personalities home—to *you*, the person waiting for someone to breeze through the door and cheerily call out, as Desi always did, "Lucy, I'm home!"

Fat chance.

Moving along to a busy call day, that denotes a day when the calls keep coming in and the ambulances/rescues or fire trucks keep going

sional non-critical one,
for a call. That's hypervig-
, and it goes with the job. Even
an anticipatory one-eye-open kind
our firefighter says they slept all night.
sleep, it's on-edge, waiting-for-a-call sleep.
son the hard way. I would call Jeff first thing in
ask, "Did you sleep last night?" The answer to this
, along with the tone of his voice, would tell me what kind
e were going to have. Early in our marriage, if he said he'd
, I would think, "Cool! We're going to have a good day." However,
that's not always the case, and it caused arguments. I would say, "But
you slept—why are you so tired?"

On busy days, there are many calls, and some of them are always
serious calls. Anything termed a serious call is taken very seriously,
because at least 10 percent of them could turn out to be critical, matters of life and death. On the other hand, many of the calls are BS calls
(and firefighters put this even more strongly—no surprise there). In
a nutshell: you simply would not believe the ridiculous things people
call 911 for.

Someone might call at two in the morning to say they feel ill and
need help immediately. Then it turns out they have the flu, have had
the flu for three whole days, and are well on the way to getting better.
This ends with an adrenaline-charged firefighter thinking furiously,
Are you kidding? I could be sleeping! In a way, these nuisance calls are
harder to deal with than the serious calls, because with a serious call,
you go into full-out work mode. You know what has to be done and
you do it. With a BS call, you feel a surge with no action mode to

follow, just frustration and irritation.

All this means that the busier the shift, the more it affects the firefighter, who has been in fight-or-flight mode—work brain mode— for the past twenty-four hours or more upon arriving at home, sweet home. A firefighter in work brain mode is fast and funny, with laser-sharp attention. Work brain is flooded with adrenaline, with an increased heart rate, a sharper sense of being alive. But when the body is working at such overdrive, such *biological* overdrive, there is only one way for it to go. And that way is *down*, into exhaustion and crashing. So, now we have home brain hitting that downward slope; it can be hypervigilant and hypercritical, noticing every little thing out of place, every detail that doesn't feel right. At our house, I always felt like we were waiting for an inspection the minute Jeff walked in the door.

Home brain can be a colossal pain in the butt.

I always joke with my husband that I was tricked because I met him on the job, which meant I fell in love with Work Jeff but married Home Jeff. As a newlywed, it didn't take long before I started thinking, "Hey! I want Work Jeff to come home. Work Jeff is *amazing*. Work Jeff is funny. Work Jeff has got lots of energy. Work Jeff doesn't have anger issues. Work Jeff doesn't bite people's heads off."

How about you? If you don't grasp the work brain versus home brain concept, you end up, as I did then, taking it personally and feeling both defiant and depressed.

And then there's fire season.

At some point, when we were first dating, I asked Jeff innocently, "What's fire season?"

Fire season is that period in the summer when fires are more likely to break out on a regular basis. Big fires. Dangerous fires. Fires that burn for days and weeks, even months. Fires that are more likely to result in both civilian and line of duty deaths. New issues firefighters have had to deal with are natural disasters, like the Montecito mudslides, hurricanes, and the Oroville Dam break.

Fire season, for readers who aren't significant others, doesn't always mean you're off fighting some exciting, apocalyptic fire. It can mean that you are sent on a strike team, overhead assignment, part of an Incident Management Team (IMT), or backfilling in the stations to make up for the firefighters who have been sent out.

Some people really enjoy going out and spend a significant amount of time getting special qualifications for it. Others prefer to stay close to home and do overtime by covering the necessary shifts. When firefighters are out at large incidents, the IMT is charged with setting up a site for all the responding agencies to meet, eat, and sleep. This is called the Incident Command Post (ICP), or fire camp. Fire camp is set up for a very special occasion and not everyone goes, even though, as I'll explain, it still affects everyone on the job deeply.

So, let's take a look at fire season and why it takes firefighters both up (those doing what they signed on to do, in the most intense way) and down (those not going out but being left at the station, or sent to hold the fort at another station). Firefighting is all about qualifications, and some firefighters have qualified to be on a strike team or on overhead assignments to go out to fires. Overhead assignments, or single resource, is when a firefighter has a specific qualification to perform a job within fire camp—logistic, line medic, communication, etc. Overhead assignments don't need an entire strike team. A single person can be sent to fill these needs.

Deployment to a large incident can last anywhere from fourteen to twenty-one days, so even if your significant other isn't off on a deployment, their work is grueling, because it requires pulling extra shifts (forget that Fourth of July party right now!) and dealing with even more BS calls.

Some stations are relatively quiet during fire season. This could be because the station isn't in a large department, so they don't send many firefighters to large incidents, due to the need for maintaining coverage in their own city. But in most stations, even if they're quiet, in terms of not being in a high fire zone, fire season is still extra stressful, because when some crew members get called out for a fire assignment, the ones left to backfill can get what we call "forced" or "mandatoried."

If you are even relatively close to someone who works within the fire service, I'm sure that you have heard all too many times about them being "forced." Because firefighting is an emergency service, the stations can't be unstaffed, since they still need to respond to local emergencies. This is referred to as "constant staffing." So, if a firefighter had plans for a day off, and a strike team from their department gets sent out, that firefighter will more than likely get forced back to work, regardless of any plans they may have made. And believe me when I say your firefighter *hates* having to make that phone call home to tell you that. My husband usually starts the call with, "You know how much I love you, right?"

Fire season doesn't care if you made plans or have a vacation you have been planning all year. One of the biggest complaints I hear from the firefighters is about the number of forces/mandatories they deal with. Some departments even have a "no days off" or set staffing patterns policy for fire season.

I've met some significant others who viewed their firefighters' time at fire camp as being off "camping." Not on your life. It's working in unhealthy breathing conditions, for hours on end, then hoping to get back to the camp setup in time to make the tail end of the dinner line and eat something before catching a little sleep. There is an entire business sector dedicated to serving the needs of fire camps—repurposing huge semis to serve as bunkhouses, catering to long chow lines, setting up communications, and generally turning fire camps into villages, much like armed forces encampments. In hard-to-reach areas, the firefighters are in actual tents for the duration. Whether in trailer or tent, some firefighters are so done in by the end of their exhausting, long workdays that they fall asleep fully dressed, not even bothering to shower the ashes and grime off their faces.

And the public watches them on TV, and sees them not just as heroes but as glamorous and sexy. That public doesn't live with one!

Living with a firefighter during fire season is far from glam. Familywise, it's hard on everyone, especially significant others with small children. You end up trying to do everything, all the time, without help. I always say I'm a "single married person." My life is like that of a single woman, much of the time, yet I'm not single and carefree.

So, with disappointed partners and sad kids missing their firefighter or feeling hurt that Mom or Dad can't show up for their game, their play, or their graduation, firefighters are never without guilt. Either they feel they're letting the crew down, or they're sure they're letting their family down. Home family or work family—someone always gets let down.

Much of a firefighter's identity is locked into their work family role, to the point where some can't disengage at all. Like a bigamist, a firefighter tends to unconsciously feel they're cheating on one family or another.

I work with cops, too, and it's not quite the same for them in this regard. Those who choose law enforcement don't always work together—they'll work alone or in pairs, or with a revolving group of other cops, so they're not as closely tied in with groups of co-workers. Still, when they get home, their behavior is much the same as firefighters', the result of adrenaline fatigue and the frustration of dealing with people who are ungrateful, judgmental, disrespectful, and who make bad choices, in the hope that the cop will fix it or maybe look the other way. Law enforcement definitely has to deal with public scrutiny much more than the fire service does. However, the one thing both struggle with is the transition from work brain to home brain.

Why Your Firefighter Acts Like a Jerk and Drives You Crazy

Firefighters come home and they're impatient without even realizing it. Everything at work is time-sensitive, so they never want the intro and the details. It's all "cut to the chase" with them, and they're puzzled when their significant other feels slighted. They usually haven't a clue that home brain requires different behavioral patterns than work brain.

It's easy to get sucked into thinking or believing it's about you or your relationship. It is very important that you remind yourself daily that this is about work brain bleeding into your home life.

Yes, it can feel like your firefighter is self-centered and dismissive of your concerns; that's because this is how it works on the job: get to the big stuff, take care of the urgencies, ignore the small stuff, and get on with it. Firefighters are puzzled when I remind them that while they are out fighting fires, running calls (whether they're BS or serious), or stuck in fire camp for days, their significant others are at home, gutting it out, so they can have their cake and eat it too—so they can have their dream job and a beautiful house, spouse, and kids. As a spouse, I have told my husband several times, "I know what I signed up for and I am willing to sacrifice, but a 'Thank you, I appreciate what you do' goes a long way."

A good example of that happened when I was deployed to the Montecito mudslides. I talked to about 350 fire personnel, educating them about mental health and the signs and symptoms they had to be aware of. At the end, I told them about saying thank you and how important it was.

After we were done, I had so many firefighters walk up to me and say, "I guess I have forgotten to say that enough." The next day, more than five guys walked up to me and said, "After your talk yesterday, I called my wife and told her thank you, and that I loved her, and she started crying."

It's easy to get wrapped up in the day-to-day stuff of life, and we all forget sometimes that simple things like saying thank you can make a huge difference. For firefighters, that also means not forgetting about all the sacrifices their significant others make due to the lifestyle. Occasionally, when I tell them they should just say "Thank you" once in a while, the response is a shocked, "Oh, I never thought about that!" or, "I forget about that sometimes."

Seriously, they have no idea they're not the same at home as at work. They don't have a clue that they're acting like jerks or being emotionally detached. Instead, when they walk through the door with that hypervigilant work brain still turned on, they immediately notice what's out of place.

I am going to give up a spouse secret right now. Depending on how old your kids are, there is a ritual we all do, starting anywhere between six and ten p.m. We round up the children and say, "Your dad/ mom will be home tomorrow, so you need to get this house cleaned up. Everyone go!" The best-case scenario for me was when my husband would call and say he had to work overtime the next day. I would tell the kids, "Hey, false alarm, everyone! Abort mission! Dad works tomorrow." We all realized that Dad coming home meant it was time for the kids and me to run around, cleaning. Then I'd walk around and inspect, thinking, *Okay, all right, we're good. He isn't going to find anything wrong this time.*

Do you think I have ever been right on this one? Sure enough, when he got home, he'd find something that was out of whack or where it wasn't supposed to be.

The funniest experience I recall was when he returned from a fourteen-day assignment in Northern California. As usual, we were all excited for him to come home, but knew he would be in total work mode with his work brain out of control. When we passed inspection on his arrival, I was feeling pretty good. One of the things my husband likes to do to unwind is yardwork. He was out working in the backyard, and I was upstairs working out, when my son came up and warned me, "Dad's in a mood."

You know what "mood" I'm talking about, right? It's that tone in their voice and look in their eyes.

Soon after, here comes Jeff. I was ready for whatever he was going to ask me, thinking I had heard it all from him before—until he walked up, looked me in the eyes, and, in all seriousness, asked, "Babe, where's my chain saw? It's not where I left it."

"Really? When have you even seen me use a chain saw?" I asked.

Of course, he wasn't hearing anything I said. He was way too focused on what he perceived as an item being out of place: "I left it in the spot in the corner where it always is, and it's not there." I mean, *just dead serious.*

"Are you joking right now?" I asked. His *chain saw.* "You're nuts. You're literally nuts. In all these years, when have you seen me with your chain saw?"

He went off, in a huff, and twenty minutes later, I heard *Revvvvvvvv.* Yeah, his chain saw.

The funniest thing? When I tell a firefighter to curb doing or saying stuff like that, the response is often, "Oh, you must have talked to my wife!" *No, dude, I don't need to. I've lived it.*

Here's the big thing you have to accept: they're brainwashed.

I don't mean this as an insult. It's simply the truth. In the fire world, there is a process for *everything.* The rest of us, we're just humans. We don't have a process for everything, so to them, *we* often seem to be the strange ones, with our messy emotions and (in their minds) odd expectations. Like every family should invariably expect to lack the presence of one family member at Christmas or Easter or Hanukkah dinner—right?

Hypervigilance is closely tied to burnout. "Burnout" might sound like a play on words when applied to those in the fire service, but it's far from a laughing matter. The classic description is that it's the state that occurs when perceived demands outweigh perceived resources. In 1996, at a seminar on trauma, the condition was described by traumatic stress and compassion fatigue expert Eric Gentry this way:

Perceived Threat = Fight/Flight =
Sympathetic Response + Chronic Anxious Presence + BURNOUT

Yikes, right? I'll break it down.

It's Not Jerkiness, It's Science

A perceived threat is something we can learn to detect through experience. A learned threat refers to something we can learn to be sensitive to from movies, books, or the news.

Let's look at an example. Whenever I watch a movie and a woman is walking to her car in a covered parking lot or underground parking structure, I know something bad will happen. I have never experienced this personally, nor do I know anyone this has happened to. However, every time I walk in a parking garage, I get scared. I am extremely alert to my surroundings, and my heart rate goes up.

If nothing bad has ever happened to me in this situation, where did I learn to be afraid of it? Obviously, from movies, books, or the news. My brain has created a slide that gets filed and pulled every time I come near a parking structure. And that slide says, "Perceived Threat."

An experienced threat is based on actual events you have witnessed personally. Let's stop and think about the calls your firefighter has told you about or even heard about from another firefighter. A baby drowning, a teenager crashing a car, a Christmas tree burning a house down? All these threats can lead to too many stress hormones and too little ability to take in the world as it really is—seeing things through the lens of learned or experienced threats and failing to see the reality.

Learned or experienced threats are all seen similarly by the brain. If you believe it to be a threat, your brain will respond, regardless of its validity. Additionally, the brain doesn't understand that "Oh, you're not at work, so it's no longer a threat." Firefighters can't turn off what they have seen.

How long your firefighter has been on the job will determine how many slides they have stored. They have the book on all the horrible things that can happen to people they love. This translates into controlling and overprotectiveness.

Any perceived or learned threat increases heart rate, breathing rate, muscle tension, and energy. Conversely, it also increases fatigue. Psychologically, perceived threat causes "dis-ease," and an inability to relax, along with obsession, compulsion, and restricted thoughts and behavior. At the same time, perceived threat decreases frontal lobe activity, fine motor control, and emotional regulation. In plain language, that means it affects language, speech, strength, speed, and agility.

Here's an example from my own life. When we bought our first house, I wanted the biggest Christmas tree they sold. Reluctantly, my husband agreed. I proudly walked out of the tree farm feeling victorious. However, I had no clue that my husband was going to obsess over it being watered and the moisture of each pine needle, nor that he would take the ugliest rope and tie it around the tree to anchor it to the wall. Of course, I was annoyed and unhappy that he made my tree look ugly. It didn't look like a Pinterest tree at all! What I didn't realize was that he worried all the time about it catching fire and burning our house down—or, worse, killing us all.

Since then, it's been fake trees for us. And what all this means is that firefighters undergo both physical and mental stresses as part of the very nature of their daily work. And yet, they love their job. Like undercover cops, fighter pilots, or brain surgeons, they have chosen a path that is always dangerous, always pressured, and at the same time, always a rush.

All of these careers have a tendency to make their practitioners view things in terms of winning or losing. This is definitely not the norm. Most people go to work and they have a good day, an okay day, or a bad day. And nobody dies.

But when you've chosen a high-risk, intense career, you have to live with split-second decisions, extremely focused concentration, and the fact that your work doesn't result in some type of personal best but directly impacts the lives or deaths or others. Pretty heavy, yes?

It's easy for people to forget that the heroic picture you see on the news or in the paper isn't the end of the story. What happens after the photo is taken? Think how many times you can remember watching the news or social media and seeing an emotional and moving picture of a first responder rescuing someone, a picture that says so much it makes you cry. When you read or hear the story, and find out everything turned out well, and the person survived, you sigh in relief and think, *Thank God, it's okay,* and move on from that story. Why wouldn't you? No one died, so the firefighter did the job well.

Well, I'm here to tell you that isn't always the case. Firefighters are trained to win all the time. If they are losing on the job, it means a house is burning down, a wildfire is raging out of control, or, in the worst case, someone is dying.

Anyone remember baby Jessica in 1987? She was stuck in a backyard well for sixty hours. The news captured the firefighter as he came out of the well with the baby. It was on the news every day, and he was on several talk shows, talking about his experience. But did you know that he quit working as a firefighter and then committed suicide?

I really want you to understand that just because the call turned out well doesn't mean your firefighter won't be affected.

I experienced this the first year Jeff was at Long Beach as a rookie. It was November 1999, and I had just put my son Kyle, who was one year old, down for his nap. Naptime was my quiet time.

Jeff called. He was really upset, and said, "I want to talk to the baby." Confused, I said he was asleep. Jeff said, "I don't care. I need to talk to him." The tone of his voice was so weird, I knew right then that something was wrong. I asked him what had happened. As I was walking to wake up our son, Jeff started telling me. At first it didn't make sense, because he was talking so fast. I got Kyle up and put the phone on speaker because Kyle was just a baby. Jeff talked to Kyle, telling him how much he loved him. I could hear his voice cracking. Then, finally, he explained what had happened.

It was a house fire. The elderly man who lived there told the firefighters that no one else was in the house. They started putting the fire out, and Jeff said he was in a room that was filled with so much smoke that he could barely see anything. He was pulling the ceiling—which means using a fancy tool and pulling the celling down to expose the structure. He told me he heard a weird noise, his gut telling me it wasn't good. He dropped to his knees and started crawling, searching for the source.

What he found was a little boy, under a bed, surrounded by clothing. He grabbed the child and ran out of the house. As soon as he hit the grass he pulled his mask off and started CPR. The little boy wasn't breathing. The picture you see here is my husband with the child in his arms rushing him to the rescue vehicle.

An important part of this story is why our firefighters are all affected differently, based on what personal life stage their family is at. Our son Kyle was six months younger than the little boy in my husband's arms, the little boy he was afraid would die. Look at the picture, look at how my husband is holding the little boy, and ask yourself if he is holding that little boy or our son. Now look at Jeff's face. What do you see in his eyes? Even without knowing him, I think you can feel his pain and his desperation to save this child.

He succeeded: the little boy started breathing on the way to the hospital, and went home eighteen days later. In fact, Jeff and his crew took him home in the fire truck.

Happy ending, right? Why would we think twice about any negative effects on my husband?

Jeff thought about that call for a long time. He would tell me about it and talk about it all the time. He often wondered, *What if I didn't hear him? What if we didn't get him breathing? I shouldn't have taken the word of the old man, and we should've searched better.* This went on and on, for months and months. One reason was because in the following year, Jeff was singled out and given three different awards for saving the boy's life. That kept the story alive in his memory, as did the fact that he wasn't on that call alone, and there were several other firefighters there helping who were part of that boy's survival. This created guilt in my husband's mind, because firefighters don't do this job for awards—they do it because they love it.

My point? The story ended happily, but it had a lasting, negative effect on my husband. If you are involved with a firefighter, don't ever be fooled, when a serious call ends well, into believing that your firefighter isn't still thinking about it all the time and hasn't been deeply affected by it.

Lost in all of this is often the fact that there are significant others whose lives are also impacted, and whose very real problems, trauma, and unhappiness are not only not being dealt with, but are often not even acknowledged or recognized by their firefighters, because that's not the way their minds work anymore. Their minds work in a fire world way, not in a normal person's world way.

When I was young and first married, sitting at home with two kids, fighting off loneliness, feeling both proud of my husband and resentful of feeling so out of it in terms of many facets of his life, I didn't get it at all.

If you don't understand the scientific, medical root causes of a firefighter's challenges, you can't properly define what the trouble is in your relationship, much less how to manage it. If you're like I was, and don't know any better, you think the cause just might be *you*: that you're a terrible partner, that you're a failure at marriage, that if you're not on a highway to hell, you're at the very least headed down a driveway to divorce.

So, what can you do?

In the next chapters, we'll look more closely at exactly how all these stresses affect a firefighter's closest relationships and endanger the most important one of all: *yours*.

Right now, you might feel that there is no solution other than to try to keep your mouth shut and your profile low, or to resign yourself to endless fights and bickering. But there is a solution, and once we define your biggest challenges, you'll be able to work on that solution, know how to get your partner's help, and live happily—and never ever boringly—with your firefighter.

It *can* be done.

Jeff on the Fire Family World

It's the greatest job in the world. It can bring unmatched satisfaction and the feeling of accomplishment, under the right circumstances. But those moments can be few and far between.

Preparation is key. Knowing where all of your tools are stored and that they are ready to function is critical. You can't spend valuable time searching for tools when you need them. They are stored and ready to go. The motto of my IMT is "In readiness is all." We take that seriously, being ready to conquer whatever is thrown at us. The readiness and preparation are ingrained in you starting from the first day of drill school. It becomes part of you, on and off duty. That's where it can become a bit problematic.

Yes, the chain saw story is true. But we need that kind of mentality in order to be successful. And when I say successful, I mean not only for the call, but for your career. A "normal" person doesn't function that way. What works for a normal person can be a disaster for a firefight. If what you need is stored close to where it was last time is good enough this time...that's not the same. If it's almost ready to be used now, then that's good enough...but it's not the same. If I've almost got everything done, that should be good enough...not the same.

It's tough for us to turn it off, especially in the amount of time it takes to drive home. It's not a light switch. My wife often jokes that I can't sit still, especially my first day off. It's even worse coming home from a team assignment. Spending weeks in the same pattern— being on your game each and every day, being able to relay and convey directions to other firefighters—it doesn't just go away when you pull out of the station. You are in a groove. It usually takes two or three days of "letting go" before I feel like I can really relax. By then, it may be time to go back on regular shift work—and the cycle continues.

So, walking in the door at home can be tough. We know we have been away and that you have handled a lot of things. We know that we missed a game or play or birthday party. We don't feel good about it, at all. We have the regular guilt. We have the guilt of wanting to make it better. We have the guilt of wanting to tell you it won't happen again. But I don't use those words. Because then you build false hope, and that's an even bigger disappointment.

We know that you have talked to the kids. We know that you have secrets about us, and that you whisper them in front of us. That doesn't really help. We know we have let you down by not being there. We know that you have some resentment and anger and disappointment. The last thing we want is for it to continue. It would be great to cross the threshold and have it all be good. Nope, not gonna happen. It's a challenge. To not be so hypervigilant that we pick things apart. To not be so high-strung and "on task." But like I said, it's not a light switch.

It's complicated. I'm guilty, sad, disappointed, and even resentful that you got to do all these things while I was working. While I was working, you were off having fun and jackassing around. And from my perspective, you didn't even ask how my day was. What I did. Did it go well?

You want me to just blend right into the "normal" day, maybe go to some snot-nosed kid's birthday party with people I don't know when all I want to do is sit on the couch and relax... *Okay, nap!* And probably have a beer. So, you can see, there's going to be some conflict. Navigating through this is tough. Because at the same time I do want to participate, I can't—I haven't shut it off yet, or even shut it down into a lower gear. The "letdown" from a long shift or IMT assignment is a process. Everyone deals with it a little differently. And it's delicate. Same thing with the "ramp up." Take the team's on-call week, when I'm anxiously waiting for the Santa Anas to surface, to get that good-going fire. To use the skills I've trained so hard for. To really apply everything. To test myself and my crew. To perform at the absolute top of my game. The anticipation. The excitement. "Why are you so excited to leave us?" *Wait...what?* That's not it...I just...this fire...

And there it is, another glitch in the perfect world of a fire family. It's not that I want to leave you. It's not that I want to miss stuff. It's not that at all. But I do want to go do what I do. And the unfortunate part is, you can't have both at the same time. Welcome to the world of the fire family.

CHAPTER TWO

The Fire Down Below:
The Firefighter's Life Cycle And Burnout

WHEREAS MOST PEOPLE'S LIFE CYCLE CHARTS go straight from work to retirement, decades later (unless they switch vocations), a firefighter's life cycle has distinct phases that begin even before starting at the academy and continue after retirement. These life cycle phases deeply affect you, because they so strongly affect your firefighter. This chapter is about "the fire down below," the stresses faced throughout a firefighting career—stresses buried so deeply that both you and your firefighter might not even be aware of them.

Getting to Stage One

The stress starts as soon as a young man or woman with a dream puts in an application to a department. Applying to a department isn't just about paperwork. Applicants have to go through rigorous testing that starts with up to hundreds or thousands of applicants. As with all fire service tests, acceptance guarantees very little, as a certain grade must be attained on every single test to continue. Otherwise, too bad, my friend, you're out until the next time you're allowed to apply.

Those who pass the written test go on to the physical agility test. Depending on the department you're applying for, there are several different forms and names for this test, and some larger departments may have their own. This extremely challenging physical test requires the candidate to go through various stations, completing several physical tasks, like hose carries, climbing a tower with a hose pack, or dragging a dummy that weighs about 160 pounds—all of them timed, of course. If the candidate passes the set standards required by the department, the next step is likely an interview panel, which can have up to three people asking various "What would you do" questions. My husband and other firefighters tell me that it's not always about having all the right answers. You need more than merely knowing what to say to get the points needed to pass. If you fail—well, you figured that part out already.

After passing the panel interview, the next step a candidate goes through is a chief's interview. Understand that you can pass the panel interview and not get to the chief's interview. If the chief's interview is passed, the department can tentatively accept the applicant. Additional steps that remain include a psychological test, with a thirty-plus-page questionnaire, and a psych evaluation. A background investigation is also conducted. This includes financial and driving statements, and visits to neighbors and former employers. Candidates are most often the same age as college applicants; getting into college might seem easy in comparison.

Acceptance to the academy is the first big step on the road to success, but there isn't much time to celebrate, not with fourteen to sixteen weeks centered on five days of twelve hours each. Nor does everything grind to a halt at the end of those twelve hours, since studying is a must. That means students study at night with those "littermates," and at home after that.

And how's this for pressure? Getting into the academy is only half the battle. Once in, an academy student can get kicked out at any time, if they fail to pass a test by a certain percentage. This is true for *every single test*, and it means that every day holds the potential for dropping out.

Firefighter candidates will already start to grow distant at home, simply because it's impossible to be emotionally present in both places. Their lives become a nonstop round of school, studying—both alone and in groups—staying late at the academy, grabbing something to eat, then going to bed. As if that weren't stressful enough, the mental game that runs through the fire service starts on day one. Similar to hazing, it's not for the overly sensitive. It's designed to toughen the students and prepare them not only for the work they will be doing but also the culture they will live in for twenty-four hours or more at a time. This is very stressful for students of any age, especially since the rank system that begins at the academy, to instill respect, can be a matter of great pride—or painful disappointment.

I've experienced the academy as both a wife and mother. Being the mother of a firefighter is even harder than being the wife. It is almost impossible to find the words to describe the fear I felt when Kyle took his first seasonal job as a forest service hotshot. He was ten hours away from home, and would be gone two weeks or more at a time with no cell service. There were nights when both my husband and son were out on fires at the same time.

I've always done a pretty good job of not obsessing over what *could* happen with my husband, but now my baby boy was out there facing these dangers. As a clinician for fire and police, I have been on several calls involving line of duty deaths. My knowledge of what *could* happen is on overdrive.

My son had been a hotshot for four weeks when I was called to respond to an incident: a hotshot had been killed by a falling tree. In the forest service world, a limb from a dead or burnt tree is called a "widowmaker," for obvious reasons. As I sat there listening to the crew talk about what they saw, all I could see was my son running for his life. I had to put that aside so I could be there for them as they grieved for their lost crew member. As a parent of a firefighter, you want to just say, "No! Why can't you be a doctor or banker, anything that doesn't put your life at risk every day?" But being a first responder is a calling—it's not what someone does, it's who they are. So I suck it up and support him, and smile in front of him but cry and worry when he's not looking, and look forward to hearing his voice whenever I can.

When my son started thinking about going into the fire service, he would ask me, "Mom, how will I ever live up to Dad's reputation?"

I told him, "You can't. You have to create your own name and reputation—but at the end of the day, a man has only his name. Protect your name in all you do." By the time Kyle was finishing out his first year, he realized that while people did know his father, they accepted Kyle as a separate person. My son feels honored to follow in his father's footsteps; it's the family business.

As soon as Kyle was laid off, after the summer, he decided to apply to other departments for a full-time job. As is usual, due to the limited number of slots, he received a lot of rejections—so he decided to put himself through an academy for more experience.

He started a twelve-week academy course and did well from the start. I was thrilled when he was promoted to commander there, especially because I knew he still felt the challenge of living up to his dad's reputation; instructors have high expectations for the son, based on the father. The fire world has fewer than Kevin Bacon's six degrees of separation. It's more like two, because even after just five or six years in the fire service, you'll know someone who knows someone else. It's a pretty small world, considering the number of people who work in it.

This is just one example of how the psychological part of the academy can sometimes be even more stressful than the physical aspects. As Kyle was finishing at the academy, he would call me every night to tell me about his day. When I'd say, "Wow, it really sounds like you're in your own spotlight," he would assure me that, yes, he was. That made all of us very happy.

The academy-rookie connection differs, depending on the department, because some academies are standalone while others are connected to departments, so that a student gets hired first and then sent to the academy. Attending a standalone academy, as Kyle chose to do, means going through the entire twelve to sixteen weeks of academy all over again, if hired after graduation by a department with its own academy. From the start, firefighting is only for those who are seriously committed to the career.

So, you graduate. You've done it. You have a job. Now you're on the team, right?

Hold your horses, kid. Now you're going to be a rookie for at least an entire year, and that means a whole year or more of proving yourself all over again. As I said earlier, the rookie has a separate rule book that is designed to make sure all rookies earn their place as full-fledged firefighters. That means plenty of chores and no taking it easy, no sitting down and watching TV with the non-rookies, or relaxing with your uniform shirt off.

After probation, as long as you pass your tests, you've earned the right to call yourself a firefighter. Maybe. You will still be the lowest man on the totem pole. That usually means you are still responsible for many of the same things you were as a rookie!

It's easy for newbies to this fire stuff to complete the rookie year and be fooled into thinking, *Whew! Now my life will be back to normal.* Guess what? It is just getting interesting.

The Firefighter's Life

The pressure doesn't let up, nor does the studying necessarily end. As soon as they attain full firefighter status, many graduates almost immediately start to work toward further qualifications. They need qualifications to be on strike teams or be considered for overhead assignments. Getting qualified as an engineer to drive the fire truck is the next step up, in many departments. In some, you can pass up an engineer's spot, but must still pass the engineer's test in order to move up in rank.

You're probably thinking, *Are you kidding me? When does it end?* But if you take a hard look at your firefighter and their personality type, I think you'll realize, if you haven't already, that most firefighters are type A personalities—overachievers who always want more.

There are exceptions, naturally, and some firefighters are content with one or two promotions. It just depends on your firefighter's personality. My husband is an overachiever, so as soon as he was able to take the next test, he did, and if there was a special project or group he could take on, he did.

While the requirements for your firefighter to advance may not be the same as the requirements for someone in a different state or even county, everything is similar. For example, when Jeff was hired at Long Beach City Fire Department, he had to start from the ground up as a boot/rookie firefighter. He had been an active paramedic/captain in his previous job, so when he passed the probation period, he was activated as a medic immediately and didn't need to requalify. But the city's fire service had a minimum requirement of six years before being allowed to study for the next promotion, which meant Jeff still had to put in his six years before he was eligible to promote to captain.

When a firefighter decides to go for promotion, it's advisable to start preparing a year in advance. So, yes, here we go again, with more time away from the family. As a side note, I figured out how to play this in order to make us closer as a family and spend more time together, too. We'll get to that in the next section of the book, so you will be able to beat that game, too.

Once firefighters pass all the required levels for promotion, their scores for all ratings are combined and tallied and they end up on the "list," in order of highest to lowest score. Where they come out on the list is *huge*, and they talk about it for weeks.

Just because they pass and make the list, that doesn't mean they will get promoted right away. It depends on the open spots for that rank. Each firefighter will get promoted in the order they fall on the list, which is why the list is critical. As firefighters move from promotion to promotion, they have to deal with long waits if they're passed over for a promotion the first time. Or the second time. Ad infinitum. And every time, the testing is rigorous, and the competition is fierce.

For example, when attempting to qualify first for captain and later for battalion chief, Jeff had to undergo an even more brutal testing process, involving both written tests and scenario-based tabletop exercises. For the latter, some departments use an actual board, while some use slide presentations, in which fire layouts are shown and the candidates must respond to the input. As with everything else in the fire service, if you have a bad test day, you're out of there and face a two-year wait to reapply.

It is *stressful* in the extreme.

Now, let's say the firefighter aces everything, including the chief's interview. What comes next is…waiting. There is a wait of two weeks or longer for the famous "list" to appear. If you've been part of a fire family for any length of time, you already know that the list is the holy grail of documents, not just because of the order of promotion, but because that's how a firefighter gets bragging rights.

Here's how it works. If there are five openings and someone comes in sixth on the list, that would be a prestigious place (say, in a field of thirty or forty). But it wouldn't bring a promotion, because there's no spot to fill. When that list gets posted, everyone wants to know, "Where did you place on the list?" And if you placed sixth, no one's going to congratulate you for what in a horse race would be the coveted "place" position—nah, they're taking the mickey, because you didn't get promoted. And you? You have to grin and bear it—the fire service isn't the place for broken hearts.

We had a good friend who placed fifth on the engineer's test, and his fellow firefighters kept sneaking the words "five" or "fifth" into every sentence! Hahaha, right? But what can seem mean to us is just a mental game for them. As a significant other, it matters that you comprehend the pressure to be high on the list as well as the need not to show disappointment if a promotion isn't achieved. It's just how it goes.

I am not forgetting about all of us significant others. What is going on in your life or your dreams and desires is my focus, and we will look at and resolve those challenges in the next section. In the meantime, let's look at what eventually waits at the end of all those tests and promotions.

Calling It Quits: Retirement

Most firefighters approach retirement with mixed feelings. On the one hand, it means the end of backbreaking work that is also mentally demanding and prompts a curtailment of anything resembling a normal life. On the other hand, it's *the life*. It's not easy to walk away.

I always advise firefighters to spend a year preparing for retirement. Why so long? Because they need to learn how to *have* a life like other people's, something they haven't done for twenty, thirty, or forty years. Some have told me, "I'm going to sleep in every day and go fishing or play golf." In theory, this sounds great, but in practice this will work for about six months before they grow bored and get tired of it. The idea of retiring and doing nothing is overwhelming at best. I always tell firefighters they need to practice what they are going to do for about a year, so that it becomes their new habit. This allows for a smoother transition and helps decrease the anxiety that can come from leaving the fire family and losing your support system of thirty-plus years.

That alone provokes anxiety: no more littermates, no more adrenaline pumping every day, no more races to the scene, no more studying, no more doing what they dreamed of then did for so long. Remember, it is who they are, not what they do. Also, be aware that if the firefighter gets seriously injured, they may get medically retired—which will completely throw them for a loop. Because not only will they lose their support system of the fire department, but now they have to deal with the workers comp side, which isn't necessarily fire-friendly in any way, shape, or form. This can translate to your firefighter being home every day without a plan, where they will take their grumpiness out on you and the family.

And while the firefighter is nervous about filling a lot of time and space after retirement, the firefighter's significant other is anxious about emptying a lot of time and space. As I said, being a firefighter's other half is like being both married and single, and now someone is going to encroach on that single territory.

As my husband gets closer to retirement, I get nervous about having him home *every* night. For our entire marriage, I have adjusted my life and how I do things based on his being gone at least ten days a month. So how is this going to work? Even now, as an "expert" on these matters, I worry about having enough to talk about, whether we will still be close and connected, if we can be around each other all that time without arguing. I have always joked with him and told him we would have to renegotiate our contract, because I didn't sign up for every night. And I am now focused on my career.

The main message here: it's important for *both* parties to plan ahead. For you, the significant other, it's as important for you to grasp how your relationship will change as it is for the firefighter to explore the options open after retirement, whether it means taking on another line of work, teaching younger firefighters, becoming a volunteer, or whatever. I have some lessons for handling this big change, too; for now, just know that the pressure doesn't simply end, not for the firefighter and not for the family.

Stresses and Strains for Everyone

Remember how I said the fire world was a whole other world? It's akin to a parallel universe at times, a world filled with sensations and stresses others can't understand. If you don't believe me, try explaining to someone else the firefighter's modus operandi and perceived threat, or work brain versus home brain. Other people don't have to deal with these, nor do they normally have partners who grow overprotective and cynical over time, or who can be physically present at home but mentally absent.

The next chapter deals with the heavy stuff: trauma, critical incidents, line of duty deaths, burnout, and PTSD. In order to better understand each of them, and to comprehend what multiplies the stress your firefighter faces during every life cycle stage, it is important to understand the concept of "perceived demand" outweighing "perceived resources." This is when burnout can start, not just for those in the fire service, but in general, for everyone. It is what happens when the demands placed on you outweigh the resources you have available, either mentally or in the form of actual equipment, that allows you to do what needs to be done.

What you perceive as a demand or as stressful may not be what I perceive as a demand or as stressful. We all have our own cup for perceived demands, and depending on how full that cup is, how much space remains when perceived demands are eating up space, that remainder equals our resources. It is individualized. A "perceived demand" is anything you perceive as filling your cup—an expectation, a stressor. When firefighters go to work, what they perceive as a demand on them varies. It depends on how full their cup already is from work, things like how many shifts they've been on, how many mandatories/forces they've had, what's going on at home; all these factors get thrown into the mix.

Now, when I talk about "perceived resources," I'm referring to both tangible pieces of equipment and a person's mental ability to handle the demands and expectations that arise. Perceived resources can be either equipment or the resources needed to cope with the challenges, like the fire truck or engine, or the equipment a firefighter uses on a daily basis to do the job. It's a reasonable expectation (for most, anyway) that your tangible resources or equipment are ready to go without your having to do anything but check things out and run your calls. When it's not, that becomes a "perceived demand," because now it stresses your firefighter.

If you show up and you're in a spare rig, you're not happy—or if the rig is broken down and everything needs to be switched out, that's no fun, either. A legit resource has been turned into a perceived demand, with added stuff to do. Or, for medics, if the medic on the previous shift didn't restock the rig, the medic might start their shift, and to them it's just not right. The resources, all the things they need to have, are screwed up. That is an unwelcome perceived demand. And what was a perceived resource turns into a perceived demand. The firefighter is starting right off, going, "Oh, great! Why do I have to start my shift like this?"—only their version of that thought is X-rated.

Equipment problems are one thing, but the other perceived resources—the firefighter's own physical and mental ability to deal with whatever's come up, their resources to deal not just with life but with calls and everything else—is equally important, if not even more. For some, the demands poured into that cup might start overflowing and pushing the resources out. If that happens, if that's how they start their day, then all it takes is one thing to send them over the top.

If we use the cup analogy as a reference, we all have one cup, some bigger than others, depending on your ability to deal with life. Now, we don't get a work cup and a life cup—we get only one for everything. Most firefighters' cups tend to be more than half-full with perceived demands at all times. They get used to and adapt to living in a dysfunctional state—but this means that their margin of error is thin. This is why sometimes it doesn't take much to make them have a meltdown over something small. That's why it doesn't have to be a big call that sends them over. And this can really get into our firefighters' heads and make them wonder if they are losing their edge or their ability to do their job.

The other situation that arises is that firefighters become so used to running at a dysfunctional level on a regular basis that they may not realize they are in trouble emotionally until it's too late, or they don't recognize the precarious status of a fellow firefighter because it's their normal state of mind. Due to this thin margin of error, it is critical that they be proactive and always work to pour some perceived demands out of the cup so they have room to fill it back up with resources.

When you have a perceived threat and your overstressed brain is bogged down by perceived demands, it doesn't know the difference between reality and perception. When a firefighter thinks something long and hard enough, the brain goes, "Okay, let's react the way we need to react. This is a threat, so we're gonna release all the adrenaline and go full-out fight or flight! We're gonna do it all!" That's because the brain is convinced that this is the necessary response.

When someone does this over and over, it wears them down, and you get burnout. Stress hormones go up, and the ability to take in the world as it really is goes down. Anyone who nodded empathetically when I admitted my fear in parking garages knows how that feels. Your body reacts to the perceived threat, you get into fight-or-flight mode, and your heart rate goes up. So now you're suddenly both more alert *and* scared to death. The worst-case scenario never came true for you, but your brain believes it will, so your body reacts. And as that happens, your ability to look around and think, *Oh, nothing's actually going to happen, there's no one here* decreases. You lose that ability.

My husband has the "Christmas tree that burns down the house" scenario. A firefighter who has been called to the scene of a baby drowning might get nervous about pool parties for the kids and make the whole family anxious with questions about who is going to be there, how deep the pool is, and whether the kids will be supervised 100 percent of the time.

These are legitimate fears that have been stored away. Firefighters call them slides that they store in their memories, of all the calls they have run in their careers. When you think about your partners, all the years they have been in this field, and how many calls they've run, you have to consider how many perceived threats they have filed away. This is why I always say that firefighters have an encyclopedia of all the bad things that can happen to the people they love. They have this entire encyclopedia stored in their brains, all this info about the many weird ways in which you can die—and that tends to make them more protective, a little OCD, a little controlling about their environment, because they know what can happen when you don't have control.

When Jeff and I started dating, we had pagers instead of cell phones (I know, I'm old), and he would insist that I page him with a code so he knew I had made it safely to wherever I was going. My stubborn nature makes me fight rules like this. I would do it, but with attitude. Irritated, I would argue that I didn't need to check in all the time. I jokingly call him my PO (probation officer) because I had to make sure I checked in constantly. Finally, I asked, "Why do you need me to check in when I leave and when I arrive?"

He answered, "Because something bad could happen to you, and I need to know you're safe." The *need* part was what I heard as important. Now that we have cell phones, it does make it easier, but it is also easier for him to obsess about my safety.

The other ritual he has insisted on is a phone call in the morning and at night. I tried to fight this one, too, but gave in when I realized that firefighting is very unpredictable, and for us to hear each other's voice or for the kids to talk to their dad every day was beyond important.

We all know that we can't really control our environment. But for firefighters, it's as if a voice keeps telling them, *You have to make life safe for your family, and you can do it because you can see all the things that could happen.*

Remember, this is what occurs biologically for the work brain. When firefighters are at work, they don't have to be on a call in order to be hypervigilant, because there is always the anticipation of a call. You're at work, you have to be ready. Period.

Work brain puts firefighters into that hypervigilant state where their bodies keep releasing adrenaline because they're always anticipating a problem. Work brain firefighters are energetic and alert, having a great time. But that hypervigilance makes them behave differently with the family. Why? Because they fear for the family. Firefighters who arrive home when work brain is still turned on aren't having fun like they are at work. They're split, and it's easy for us, their significant others, to think, *Hey, why are you different when you're here? Those guys, do you like them better than me?*

It's not easy for normal people to understand—or for many firefighters to grasp—how that adrenaline surging results in being fun at work and being a drag at home. But it isn't just some kind of bad mood—it's a physical and chemical reaction. It's not unusual for a firefighter to walk in the door and announce, "I'm just going to sit down for a minute," because they are rapidly coming off that adrenaline, and it's such a hard crash that they physically can't do anything else. They want to, mentally, but physically they're so exhausted that the minute they stop moving, they're out like a light. My husband says, "If I stop moving, I can't keep my eyes open. But if I keep going, I can stay awake."

The only cure is time. It takes eighteen to twenty-four hours for the body to get back to a normal state. If they go back to work the next day, there isn't always enough time for their bodies and minds to get completely out of work brain. A transition period between work and home gives your firefighter a chance to adapt. Gradually, as with a dimmer switch, the adrenaline stops crashing after the surge and gets back into the normal range. The body, physiologically, needs time to adjust.

Both physically and emotionally, calls they had that day also impact how they feel and act. Did they have to cut somebody out of a car? Did they do CPR on an infant? Whatever they did that day keeps their brain going, so they don't get to come off of it right away, but get stuck in work brain and need to transition.

It isn't only adrenaline, either. Feelings have an impact. Firefighters might be feeling many emotions from their day, but they don't want to process the emotion because it's a lot of work, so they leave it locked up. This is why you get the unemotional person who is there in body but not in spirit—because they have automatically decided to deal with the emotions later. But then they go to work and don't deal with them there, either. And maybe they run five more calls, traumatic calls, to store in that locker, to "deal with" later. They want to spend time with their partner, their family at home. So they don't deal. And when they walk in the door, knowing we need them to be engaged, even though they're exhausted, they don't want to let us down yet again, so they stay in work brain and push through. That means they approach us, the kids, or any task from a work brain perspective, which leaves out any emotional connection. It's really a lose-lose for them, but they try and make the best of it.

This is why that transition period is so important. The other thing that is hard—especially if you have been waiting for them to get home and give you some help with the kids and house—but that you have to accept, as I have—is that Day One is a wash. That means it is not a day for big plans or expectations. You never know what mood they are going to be in, so it's senseless to set yourself up to be let down or disappointed yet again.

Paradoxically, their overprotectiveness toward the family often makes life uncomfortable for the rest of us. Eager to keep their home a sanctuary, they can make it seem more like a prison (as I mentioned earlier, Jeff was once known as the Funsucker by the kids and me). But, again, it's not a matter of being a jerk—it's the result of trauma and that difficulty in shifting from work brain to home brain.

What's the lesson in all this? As we go on to the next chapters, it's important to do so with a full understanding of not just the critical but also the everyday firefighter stresses. Firefighting will never be "just another job," because all first responders have to deal with death and destruction, followed by carrying and dealing with the trauma. And that means that, to a degree, you must do the same. Only by realizing that the habits required to be a good firefighter are the same habits that can be hazardous to family happiness can you make sure your own life and well-being are not sacrificed in service to the fire world, and instead become an active partner to the firefighter you love.

The Firefighter Life Cycle from Both Sides

Even after all these years together, I don't always know what my husband is thinking. So I asked Jeff if he would write down his thoughts—about my thoughts, things that have bothered or confused me and probably some of you, too. I think the results show that, while both firefighters and significant others are poles apart on some things, most of that is simply due to not understanding how the other person is feeling or why they're acting the way they do. Please keep in mind that he and I have made it through all these phases so far, and are still happy and together. We're both a bit nervous about his future retirement, but I think we've learned enough over twenty-odd years to survive that, tóo!

Significant other thoughts and concerns	*Firefighter thoughts and concerns*
Pre-fire	
It's so hard seeing my partner get rejected over and over by departments and academies. And dealing with the anger/depression/bad mood takes its toll.	Truthfully, it sucks...so bad. All the preparation. Station visits. Practice interviews and agilities. It sucks. Period. I was so prepared. I put everything I had into it. And still got dumped out. Not fair. What did I do wrong? I nailed it. I wasn't the only one who got rejected, of course. Plenty more folks out there did, some many times over. And every time it hurts a little bit more. Then, for whatever reason, it works out. I can look back now and say that at any point one little change would have totally altered my life.
I try to stay positive for him/her, but sometimes I feel that they aren't going to get hired and then what will we do?	Like I said, it's a process. You must stay focused and not ever give up. The rejection hurts. Sets you back. Makes you wonder if it will ever happen. Have your pity party. Let it out. And get over it. Pull your boots back up and get to it. You won't get there if you aren't trying. Kind of like the lottery; you can't win if you don't play. The payoff is truly golden. Everything you thought it would be and more.
He/she says that the fire service will be a better life for us in the long run. I believe in them and I'm ready for this journey, but it's so hard at times.	The fire service allows you to provide for your family, your future, your retirement. It has such wonderful steps throughout, but it all comes with a price. More than one price, in fact. The commitment to whatever you are testing for: mock orals, practice agility, station visits, time away from the family. The reward is coming. Everything from the satisfaction of a good run to holidays with family at the station. It's a lifestyle like no other—so unique. People wonder what it's like and you (and your family) are the ones living it. Task. Purpose. End state.

Academy

Thank God the letter came: he/she made it.	Omigod, I got it. *I got it!* The golden ticket, or as my agency refers to it, the brass ring—the one you grab on a merry-go-round (yep, totally just dated myself). It's time to celebrate, though you also feel a little sorrow at leaving your old job and a little anxiety. But so excited!
I am truly excited and so proud of him/her and can't wait for them to graduate. We have T-minus sixteen weeks to go.	This will be what seems like the shortest and longest time in history. This time is so essential on both sides. The academy is demanding and grueling. You're up early and home late. Going all day long. You are forging your future and being challenged. Through peaks and valleys, you grow. And this is just the beginning of your career.
I am so excited about this journey, but I feel like such an outsider. The only way I can play a small part is by preparing food for him to take for his classmates.	What a treat! Fresh-baked goodies. Hot chili on a rainy day. Wow! So awesome. And a great way to get your significant other involved and to play a part. Rotate hosting weekend study groups so as many families can meet your littermates. Get them to buy into what you are going through, because they are, too.
With the commute and study time, I see him/her for maybe a couple hours at night. I'm trying so hard to be supportive, but I'm starting to realize this is way more than I expected it to be. Still, I don't want to burden anyone with my feelings—I know they need to focus, so I will keep it in.	There is a downside to the academy. Maybe a few. The pressure is intense, at the academy and at home. Extra study time. Maybe a slight injury. Early and late days. Having so little time with family. Having to stay focused so I don't blow this. Paying attention to the family since they are in this, too, and deserve and need the attention. But I really need to study.
What the hell...? He shaved his head to look like everyone else. Should I tell him he looks like he just joined a hardcore gang?	Most people do not understand the rituals and rites of passage. They don't get the *why*. Why do you have to learn to march? And know cadence? Does it really matter how to throw a ladder? Or stretch a line? Yes, it really does. You'll get it later.

About week eight is when I realized this was not at all what I thought I had signed up for. They now have to study on the weekends with classmates, and they just added night drills, so now they'll be home even less. It seems like the days when I'm alone are increasing a lot. I'm hoping it will get better once all this is over.

Halfway there. Cruising? Struggling. Feels kinda good, in a rhythm. Okay, not really good. It starts to wear on you: the grind, the lack of sleep. Ever wanted a nap when you got home only to find out your kid's second-grade friend has a birthday party that you have to go to? Never even met the kid. And as the end draws closer, it gets harder. More to study, to practice.

Holy crap, what just walked in my door but Satan himself! Yelling, throwing things, very angry. Turns out he failed a block test. What is a block test, and why has this become my and the kids' problem?

You will have some setbacks. No doubt. Depends on the level. Minor to major, it is still a shock. And the stakes are now elevated, because I don't want to blow it. I can't afford to blow it. I need to study more, maybe an extra night and a little on the weekend. No big deal, right? Midterm or block exams are major hurdles. *Major.* "You know if I don't pass the make-up test, I'm done, right? You wonder why I'm upset? Gimme a break."

I feel like we all have to walk on eggshells.

This brief period of time compared to the length of your career is ever so short. But ever so important. And it's easy to get hyperfocused on your goal. You can become so engrossed in the academy that you don't realize what's going on around you. Life for the rest of your family goes on. Normal people stuff. Playtime. Baseball practice and games. Whatever it is, it's easy to check out from those things. To you, the academy is the rule; to a degree, it's the only thing that matters. That has to be relayed to your friends and family. You owe it to them to keep them informed and part of the equation.

We made it to graduation and the pinning ceremony. I am beyond proud of how hard he/she worked. I got to pin my partner and it was such an honor to share that and see the joy in their eyes.

What a relief. Got through that. Piece of cake, right? Okay, not so much. You left quite a wake during the last sixteen weeks. Now you get a special day and a chance to relax for a moment and spend some time with the family. You know it will give them a false sense of security, that they will expect you to be around more. You know better, but why spoil their hope?

So glad that's over! Now things will get back to normal...

No reason to say anything. They will just adapt to the new normal. Won't they?

Rookie Year

I didn't even realize that my firefighter has a new set of "rules" as a rookie. They seem so childish and ridiculous!

Like I said, most people don't get it. These rules set the tone. Remember, it's paramilitary. There is a pecking order, the importance of rank. What other people don't see is the formation of a game plan. Learning time management. Learning to prioritize. Learning to recognize patterns of behavior.

Some days are so lonely! My partner still needs to study nights and is so tired by the end of the day that there is nothing left for me or the kids.

Remember learning about time management at the station? Now you need to work on applying it at home so you can make everyone happy (or at least try or fake it).

I don't think my firefighter understands or cares how stressful this is for me. I don't want to add any more stress to the situation so I just hold it in.

There is a bit of a division regarding the stress: neither one of you will understand where the other is coming from, and each of you has your own perspective. It is two separate worlds. I'm focusing on passing probation; you are focusing on holding down the fort. I hate dealing with it, too, but both of us have to talk about it. Keeping these things penned up doesn't do anyone any good. It just builds resentment. Firefighting is always a big stressor, and we have to deal with it.

Some days I don't think I can handle it. I've started feeling anxious before my firefighter even gets home. What personality will walk through the door? Are we going to fight again today?

This isn't an easy job, not for anyone. Add to it the trials and tribulations of probation and all the things that go with being a rookie, and it takes a lot out of you. All I want is a nap when I get home. I'm tired and a little hungry. I know the lawn needs to be mowed. I don't need to be reminded of it 500 times. I have just as much anxiety as my other half does. My anxiety goes up on the way home, too.

It was a rough year, and I'm now the significant other of a regular firefighter. I am very happy and proud. And again I'm hopeful we will now get to a normal routine.

This life isn't normal by any stretch of the imagination. That's part of the allure. It gets in the way. A lot. Believe me when I say that I as well as my family have learned more than I thought. Now a whole new horizon of opportunities lies ahead: bids, specialty training, paramedic school.

Firefighter

At this point I'm so sick of the fire service controlling every aspect of my life! I have given up on summer vacations because they always get cancelled.

Remember the learning I mentioned? Time management? Now we need to put it to use in a different light. Smaller day trips may have to take the place of the "endless summer" (fire world summer will always be endless in another way, for sure). I need to bring the family to the station for dinner, put them up in a hotel, and meet them for breakfast the next morning. We can spend the day together, then I'll go home and sleep in my own bed. I can set up an alliance network for trades and those last-minute "I need help" coverage issues. We will all likely have to bite the bullet for someone at some point, but that is how we make it work.

I give up so much. Then when my firefighter gets sent out on an overhead assignment and is so excited to leave us yet again, it breaks my heart and I feel like fire will always be more important than I am.

The excitement is not about leaving you. It's about engaging in what we love to do. It's about doing what we signed up for, about the challenge. Sure, it's exciting, that adrenaline rush. Call it a high or whatever you want. But it's not about leaving you. We can see what you're thinking in your eyes, hear it in your voice, and even read your body language. This doesn't make it any better or easier. At that moment, it is lose-lose for us. And it sucks.

My firefighter is gone so much with regular days and overtime and fire assignments for weeks on end! I want to understand this passion for the job. I love to ride out and feel a part of their fire family, and I have truly grown to love the crews— no matter what station he's at— as much as he does.

The cliché of the two families is a fact. We do things differently at the station than at home. Can any firefighter reading this relate to me in the chain saw story? If so, I strongly encourage you to interact with your own family at the station as well as at home. Show them what you do, where you sleep, everything about what your "other family" is. It's so important for them to know and be a part of it.

Now that we have kids, I call myself a single married person. He/she misses so many of their activities. I feel overwhelmed some days, doing it all by myself.

We know. We aren't fond of it, either. We know it creates extra stress. And, yes, we know the other parents are talking. One of the things I did was to get involved with the sports my kids played. Really involved, board member level. I would always ask the person doing the sports schedule to try and be flexible around my work schedule. It's never gonna be 100 percent, but when you are getting to more events than you are missing, life is better.

Many of my friends joke about my "pretend" husband because he misses so many things we get invited to. I laugh but it stings a little.	Regular people don't get it. Our lifestyle is very different. The funny thing is that these same people that poke fun at your "pretend" spouse are the ones that say, "Must be nice to have all those days off." Yeah, right. Let's get something straight. The average firefighter workweek is fifty-six hours. Average. That's sixteen hours more a week than the regular schmuck's workweek. All those days off in a row still equals less time off than other people get on average. And that isn't counting all the extra shifts.
I don't think he has a clue about how much I actually do as a stay-at-home parent. I'm not lounging around watching reality TV all day.	Bonbons and soap operas all day, right? Probably shouldn't have said that out loud. We don't recognize or acknowledge enough what goes on at the home front when we are gone. I've learned that a simple "thank you" goes a long way.
When he is at home, I know he wants to help and be a part of the family, but the kids and I have a system and a ritual like he has at work. It makes me angry and frustrated when he changes our schedule.	Double-edged sword here. We end up in a spot where we don't know what to do. You tell us you are overwhelmed when we aren't there, and when we are you complain that we mess things up by not doing it your way. Well, I never got the memo saying that's the way we do it. So, do you want my help or not?
When he/she tells me about a great call or jokes at the station, I sometimes resent my partner's career and success. I know I was part of the plan to stay home while the kids are little, but I can still feel sad about it. I don't think my firefighter grasps how much I sacrifice.	Many of us firefighters, because we live in such a black-and-white world, feel that if we made an agreement, we can't just change it. Couples are in this together and need to develop an alternate plan. Feeling resentful won't change the situation. Firefighters are fixers. But this isn't something we can just fix on our own to make all better overnight.
I hate when he/she looks at work email and then gets sucked into doing something right away or is angry for the rest of the day. Now our one day together is ruined. Thanks!	We all need to set boundaries, to walk away from the work stuff and devote time to our home family. They have waited for it. We owe it to them. We can catch up on emails at work and be angry with our work family instead.
I can't believe the group texts that never end! They love each other too much!	You do it, too. Your sewing circle of cackling hens that you are. Sometimes funny can't wait. And you think it's funny, too, when you hear the texts.
He/she is so funny and engaging at work. I wish that version of my firefighter would come home to me once in a while.	The relationships with the different families are different. As my significant other, you may not appreciate what we talk about—or understand it—because you weren't there. And don't get your feelings hurt when I act like I do at work and you don't like it. Be careful what you ask for!

Promotions and Specialty Training

Just when you think there aren't any more hours in the week to be taken from you...surprise! They have now taken on a promotion exam or specialty training like USAR, Wildland, or the Union. Does it ever end?

Nope. It doesn't and it shouldn't. Learning should never stop. Not in this job. Complacency and comfort are dangerous. Remember the draw of the job itself: the action, the challenge. That pattern should continue.

Is anything ever about me? Now I am helping him/her study for the captain's test. My jealousy is intense, but I try to hide it.

It's about us. Talk to me about what you want to do. Can we do both?

Well, the upside to helping my firefighter study for a promotion exam is that I learn a lot about what the applied-for position will entail, which makes it easier for us to talk about the job.

This does have some hidden value. When I was studying for captain, my son would set up the computer with fire problems, dropping and dragging smoke and flames and whatever onto a picture. My wife would sit on the bed with a recorder and a grade sheet. My son took pride into creating a challenge for me. My wife took great pleasure in hammering my score—a little too much, I think. It gave both of them an appreciation of what it really is that I do. For the record, my daughter didn't want any part of this. She did a ride-out with me on the rescue, but she slept through a couple runs. She had no interest at all.

Now that I am working again, I want the same support I gave him/her. I may or may not have an attitude about it, too.

Trust me, you have one. I'll give you all the support I can. It can't be a moving target, though...you are way too complicated for me to figure that out. Way. And when I do chores at home not the way you would like them done, remember that it doesn't mean I did them wrong. If you want anything done a certain way, tell me before I do it, not after—kinda like when we're in the car and I drive past a street and you say, "Oh, I would have turned there if I were you because there's a detour ahead." Really? Now you tell me?

One of the things I fell in love with about my husband was his passion and how he gives his whole heart to everything he does. I love to see how much he loves his crew and how respected he is. It makes me proud that he's mine.

This job can draw out the absolute best in your performance. It creates more drive. Firefighters must never let that passion go. We need to pass it on to others, young and old. Always do your best. Always train. Always be ready.

Retirement

Wait, what? You're going to be home every night? I have adjusted to having you home no more than ten days a month for twenty-three years. I'm worried we won't have anything to talk about.	I think I might go camping on the red (i.e., work) days at the start. Huge adjustment. Complete overhaul of what once was. While I'm not there yet, I've been told that you must have a plan. Whatever it is, I won't just retire cold.
I know I have complained about not having enough time with you, and now I'm complaining about too much time with you. But that's how it goes.	I'm used to having some free time myself. So we both will have to adjust and make this work. We can do things together, and also separately. And you can still talk like you did when I/we worked. It may take some time to get used to the new normal, but we will.
Now that the kids are grown, we have had to create a new life and routine, but I am really learning to enjoy our new time together and realizing how close we have grown through these years of ups and downs.	It's nice not having to cart the kids around all the time—yet I miss them, too. It's an adjustment, again, that may take time. It is going to take some trial and error. We will find common ground and explore it. And when we find uncommon ground, we will explore that, too. After all, I'll have plenty of time.

CHAPTER THREE
Red Alert: Compassion Fatigue and PTSD

W E ALL FACE STRESSES in our lives, yet the "normal" person rarely, if ever, has to deal with the everyday stresses a firefighter faces as described in the previous chapter. Firefighters, on the other hand, not only face those stresses on a regular basis, but also have to confront stresses that can push them past burnout into compassion fatigue and post-traumatic stress disorder (PTSD). These states are red alerts, because the next step is the breaking point, where the firefighter's equilibrium and mental health are seriously at stake, and suicide can be an outcome. In fact, according to a white paper on "Mental Health and Suicide of First Responders," based on a study by the Ruderman Family Foundation, in 2017, 103 firefighters committed suicide, compared to ninety-three who died in the line of duty. First responders are likely to suffer PTSD at a rate *five times* the national average.

Significant others and family members can help their firefighters by being able to recognize any of these emergency states of mind, as well as by helping the firefighters identify them, not just in themselves but in fellow crew members, too. Many fire departments are doing more to help identify and provide services that will hopefully decrease the problems, but for the most part, adequate behavioral health programs are not in place. The mental challenges facing firefighters were pretty much ignored for a long time. PTSD was identified as a disorder with specific, treatable symptoms only in 1980.

That might seem like ages ago, but, for comparison, social anxiety disorder was added to DSM-II (Diagnostic and Statistical Manual of Mental Disorders of the American Psychiatric Association) in 1968, and recognition of some patients' inability to adapt to socioenvironmental stressors goes back to the original DSM-I, published in 1952. Recognition of and treatment for PTSD have come a long way over the course of almost four decades, but firefighters are still too often left to fend for themselves.

As a therapist who specializes in helping first responders, and a wife whose husband has lived through the stuff of other people's nightmares, I value the opportunity to help more firefighters and their significant others both understand and recognize the signs of major stress disorders. I also want you to see how to change the way you both think about behavioral health, in order to deal with it as an everyday conscious choice, to address and maintain and to teach you both how to recover from old, stored-up memories, thus finding the paths back to your mental health and resiliency.

Before we go into each of the red alerts individually, picture that cup of resources in your mind. Now, picture it already at least half-full. Got it? Now, keep in mind, that is how firefighters start their days.

Line of Duty Death and Other Traumas

Most people don't have to deal with line of duty deaths (LODD). This category belongs almost exclusively to those in military and paramilitary organizations, the latter of which includes law enforcement and the fire service. It always hits hard, and how hard depends on your relationship with the person whose life was lost and how often it happens in your department.

But when it does happen in your department, it really hits home. If you or your firefighter haven't experienced this personally, there are a few things you need to understand about a LODD that are extremely important.

First, any LODD is difficult for the firefighter because it is a brother-/sisterhood and it never matters what patch a firefighter wears—what matters is that they are part of this larger family. As a significant other, don't be surprised if you hear on the news about the LODD of someone you don't know and find yourself worrying about your firefighter. I have on occasion found myself wondering what I would do if it were happening to me, whom I would call first, how I would tell my children. As stated earlier, we don't sit around worrying about this—we can't, as it would drive us nuts. But when it happens to someone else, it slams us right in the face that this *is* a possibility.

Second, an LODD service isn't like any other funeral you have ever been to. There are so many rituals that date back to the beginning of the fire service, I couldn't even list them all. The main thing you need to understand is that these rituals have absolutely nothing to do with us. In this situation, our role is to support our partners in whatever way they may need us to. Sadly, this happened to my fire family.

In June 2018, one of our captains at Long Beach Fire Department was killed in the line of duty. Dave Rosa was well-known, experienced, and respected, and his passing was like a knife in the heart of the LBFD. His service took a week of intense planning that kept my husband at headquarters for more than twelve hours a day, and even when his day ended, he still wanted to be there with his brothers and sisters while they grieved. They needed to be with each other. As part of the fire services grieving process, the service for the fallen is a show of respect for their lost brother or sister.

Remember, our firefighters are fixers—and this isn't something they can fix. They all have this need and desire to make it right, along with guilt, fear, anger, and the deepest level of sadness you can imagine. When Jeff would call and apologize for being so late or neglecting us, I would tell him, "Don't worry about us. Just do what you need to do to honor Dave in a way he deserved."

And lastly, they will all deal with their grief in different ways. I couldn't list every way. But you need to know that while they may experience their grief right away, it could be delayed or, in the worst-case scenario, held in and unprocessed. The main symptoms that you might see are irritability, impatience, trouble sleeping, anger or outbursts, and trouble focusing or concentrating. If I could pass on one tip, it would be talk about it rather than to try and act as if it hadn't happened. Ask your firefighter if they want to talk about it or if they need space. Remind them that you are there for them anytime they need to talk.

About a month after Dave's funeral, as I was on my way out of state, to provide support as a clinician on another line of duty death, my husband and I had a conversation about what I should expect. Was it too soon for me? Would I be able to be completely present for this other department that needed help to get through a situation so like the one our fire family was still struggling to deal with? I will never forget the look on my husband's face as we stood in the kitchen and he turned to me and said, "I always wondered how bad it could feel, and now I know."

The rest of the world thinks firefighters' significant others must worry constantly about the danger. They say, "Oh, you must be so scared every day!" But we aren't.

The hardest part of being a firefighter's partner isn't the possibility of death—it's the ongoing loneliness. Yes, the experience of our first line of duty death might be the first time we feel real, paralyzing fear. But we don't sit around and think obsessively about the danger. Nor is a line of duty death the only event that affects a firefighter's psyche.

A critical incident can be any call that has a strong emotional impact; it doesn't even have to be a "big" call. It all depends on how stressed out the firefighter has been that day, that set, that week, or over the past year. The point is that those in the fire service are always subject to a large amount of stress, and it can take just a single traumatic event to push them over the edge.

The normal reactions to trauma are numerous, and they affect every aspect of a firefighter's life. Physiological and emotional reactions include heightened anxiety, fears about the deaths of others, and self-blame, all of which contribute to sadness and irritability, as well as sudden mood swings. There are cognitive reactions, too: difficulty concentrating and making decisions that would normally be easy, having thoughts that dwell on death or on people who have died. It isn't unusual for anyone who has experienced trauma to feel confused and distracted, to be unable to think as quickly or smoothly as usual. On top of all this, there are physical reactions, ranging from headaches, nausea, and fatigue to muscle aches and pains. All these effects bring about behavioral changes: hyperactivity or an opposing tendency to inactivity, social isolation, and avoidance of activities or places that serve as reminders of the event, loss of appetite and disrupted sleep, sadness on awakening, and becoming easily startled.

A lot to deal with, yes? It's no surprise that the hypervigilance of the job creates a biological roller coaster, resulting in high energy at work and exhaustion at home, as well as an inability to relax caused by heightened awareness of dangers. The job can also result in a deep cynicism that leads a firefighter to trust no one, always looking for ulterior motives and expecting the worst from people. This is especially true during periods of added work stress, such as a prolonged fire season and long continuous periods of being force hired or mandatoried.

All the reactions I've listed above are symptoms of acute stress that fall in the range of normal reactions for a firefighter. Most of us couldn't handle it, if for no other reason than that we aren't used to it, nor have we been trained to deal with the high level of intensity that naturally comes with this job. What we forget is that the draw to this career is the adrenaline rush and always being "on." But firefighters are under endless stress—their cups already partially filled—so they are used to it and usually manage to function well enough that it doesn't greatly interfere with their work, even though, as we will see later, their families are often well aware of the effects of firefighters' hypervigilance as a reaction to perceived threats. Why? Because it interferes with their own lives.

For the firefighters themselves, the most serious reactions, the true red alerts—the conditions that can lead to clinical depression, breakdowns, drug and alcohol abuse, and suicide—are compassion fatigue and PTSD. As the significant other or family member of someone who is prone to both of these just by nature of the job, you should always be on the lookout for either to take hold of your firefighter, so you can identify it and get help.

Compassion Fatigue: The Curse of Empathy

As we discussed, burnout happens when perceived demands become so great that they overrun resources. In our cup analogy, the demands can push resources into overflowing, so the resources can no longer keep up with the stress. The resulting burnout is a state of physical, mental, and emotional exhaustion. And burnout is the first stage of the condition known as compassion fatigue. If you recall from *Chapter One*,

Perceived Threat = Fight/Flight =
Sympathetic Response + Chronic Anxious Presence + BURNOUT.

The key word above is "chronic." Burnout happens over time. The symptoms range from sleep disturbances to moodiness and interpersonal conflicts, from fatigue and an inability to bounce back to feelings that their efforts are futile and accomplishments meaningless. One reason it's so important to identify burnout is that if it's untreated—if efforts are not made to drain some of the stressors out of that cup—it will move on to a more serious condition. Or I should say, it *will* move on.

This is something you can count on. Most of the time, firefighters are able to process some of the stress they are under or the bad calls they have been on. They can begin to believe that it will always resolve itself. That false belief, added to the culture of "suck it up, buttercup," can get them in bad situations, with their cups overflowing. This is also where they seriously begin to doubt themselves and their ability to cope with the job. I have heard many of them say, "Why am I having a hard time dealing with this now, when I have dealt with much worse? What's wrong with me?"

As burnout persists, it gradually transitions by adding more serious symptoms to the toxic stew: social withdrawal and depersonalization, deep cynicism and irritability, chronic low energy and exhaustion, and a troubling sense of being underappreciated. And then, secondary or vicarious trauma comes in as the final ingredient that brings on compassion fatigue.

Compassion fatigue isn't the result of one call or a traumatic situation. It's simply being tired of caring.

Firefighters can handle stress, even acute stress. For starters, by the very nature of their work, they have a darker reference point. They know bad things can happen. Work brain allows them to take their share of horrible sights and frightening situations in stride. In addition, there are a lot of bad things they deal with that they firmly push out of the forefront of their minds, that they ignore or try to forget. In the early stages of burnout, first responders can be totally unaware it's even happening, due to their walling off so much of the bad stuff. And then the effects of secondary or vicarious trauma stress set in.

Secondary/vicarious trauma is the result of witnessing the suffering of others. It is not the province only of first responders. It can strike anyone who has no choice but to constantly observe what other people are going through: psychologists and psychiatrists, doctors and hospital workers. Again, we all have our cups and we all have stress. But because a firefighter starts every day with a cup that is half-full or close to brimming over, it isn't the same. The rest of us tend to cope better with acute stress situations such as divorce, illness, or an accident, because there is usually no vast accumulation of other stresses piling on regularly. And we don't have to deal with the constant onslaught of secondary trauma.

Secondary trauma results from the buildup of empathizing with another's suffering, then being haunted by the constant visualization of that person's experience—think of any time you have read about a devastating incident and thought, *I can't get that image out of my mind*—all of which activates the sympathetic nervous system. Chronicity comes in as this recurs, as if you're pouring hot coffee into a full cup until it surges over the rim and burns you. This is secondary trauma stress.

Every firefighter can tell you about *that* call, the one they dread responding to, the calls (and, trust me, there are more than just one) that are stored in that slideshow in their brain. Firefighters who help traumatized people don't just go home and forget about them. They can become fixated on them, reexperiencing the events of the call, using their energies to numb themselves or avoid anything that brings back the memories, wondering what they could have done differently, if what they do day in and day out makes any difference at all.

As a significant other, you may or may not notice that your firefighter is struggling. They get really good at hiding it from us. They worry about burdening us with all the bad stuff in their heads. They don't want us to have these horrible memories, so they hide it or tell us they are "fine."

When you are burdened with the suffering of others, it's easy to get tired of caring.

Here's how it works with a firefighter. When compassion fatigue grabs hold of you, you don't *want* to care anymore. Maybe you let yourself go and start looking a bit scruffy. Everything seems like too much trouble: sexual intimacy, going to the gym, eating properly, having a purpose. You can become forgetful, angry, or hypervigilant yet forgetful. Self-doubt and anxiety interrupt or prevent sound sleep. You might think you should do something about this, but you feel overwhelmed, apathetic, eaten away by self-doubt. Your life becomes a list of things you used to enjoy, used to spend time doing.

Now you can't be bothered. Now you make excuses not to go places with your significant other. You avoid your family. You try to avoid any calls that might be critical and anything at all that might remind you of the event that keeps flashing before your eyes. And you're obsessed with those who have suffered loss to the point that they're always with you, ghosts haunting your waking and sleeping moments.

You can't turn off the thoughts. You worry that you're weak, that you are no longer fit to serve.

You are neither. You're just in the grip of compassion fatigue.

This is a red alert. If you see these signs in your firefighter, they need help. You can start to help right now, in fact, by giving them this chapter to read because they need to recognize the signs in themselves and others they work with. They need to know how and where to get help and how to help themselves in preventing burnout, compassion fatigue, and PTSD.

Post-traumatic Stress Disorder:
When You Can't Stop Reliving the Nightmare

Post-traumatic stress is a normal reaction to any event that threatens violence or the loss of life. You may personally experience the event, or see the event happen to someone else. One of the biggest differences for first responders is having direct exposure to graphic details of the event after the fact. This stress doesn't necessarily turn into a disorder.

I'm not sure if any of you have heard of PTSI, a new term we are using with first responders. The "I" stands for injury. Think of it like a broken leg. It takes six weeks to heal, you go to physical therapy, and then are usually ready to go back to work. PTSI does impair our ability to function, but usually only for a limited time. In other words, we get over it or it affects our lives in only a certain capacity. Perhaps we have bad dreams, or are irritable, or we might feel guilty or not interested in our usual pastimes.

But when a trauma causes full-blown PTSD, as it can at any time with first responders or active duty servicemen, it causes at least *nine* separate symptoms, including those listed above, as well as sustained negative emotional states, detachment from others, reckless and self-destructive behavior, severe hypervigilance, and an inability to control verbal outbursts and irritability.

There are three different traumatic stress gradations:

Post-traumatic stress, resulting from PTSI, which can be of any duration and minimally impairs daily functioning, always features one or more symptoms in any of these areas: intrusive thoughts, avoidance, altered mood and cognition, and arousal and reactivity. Most first responders experience this one.

Post-traumatic stress, or PTSI, is like the common cold. Everyone gets sick occasionally, with symptoms lasting a few days, but it goes away and you will feel better and get back to your regular schedule. However, if you don't start to feel better, the doctor will tell you after seven days, if you're still sick, to come in and get some medication. If you don't treat the persistent symptoms, you will get sicker.

Acute stress disorder, which lasts from three days to one month and impairs daily functioning, involves nine or more symptoms in any of the above areas.

I hate to beat a dead horse about this, but if your kids were sick for two weeks, would you just tell them to suck it up and that they can make themselves feel better if they try harder? Probably not. So why would we think that thought process would work in this situation? This is where our first responders need to seek help and find a culturally competent clinician who can help firefighters process their trauma.

Post-traumatic stress disorder lasts thirty days or longer on a consistent daily basis and impairs daily functioning. To be diagnosed with PTSD, the person must exhibit symptoms in all areas.

Post-traumatic Stress/PTSI	Acute Stress Disorder	Post-traumatic Stress Disorder
• Any duration • Minimally impaired daily function	• Last 3 days to 1 month • Impaired daily function	• Last 30 days or longer consistently • Impaired daily functioning • Symptoms in all areas
One or more symptoms in any area	9 or more symptoms in any area	Intrusive thoughts (1 symptom) Avoidance (1 symptom) Altered mood and cognition (at least 2 symptoms) Arousal and reactivity (at least 2 symptoms)

The most important thing you need to understand is that to acquire PTSD you must have these symptoms for thirty days, every day, with severe impairment in your daily life. When I teach firefighters about PTSD, I ask them: when you run a call in the middle of the night for flulike symptoms, and you feel extremely frustrated, what's the first question you ask? How long they have been sick? The patient, more times than not, will say they've been sick for at least three days. This is one of the most frustrating things for our first responders. They will proceed with a lecture: why haven't you gone to the doctor? You need to take care of yourself. Now think about PTSD, and that it takes thirty days to be diagnosed with it. This needs to change, and the goal is to get all first responders and their significant others more educated, to get the help they need earlier to decrease the negative impact on their lives and the relationships they value.

If you are wondering where compassion fatigue fits in, the line between it and PTSD is a fine one. In both cases, the condition is the result of *cumulative* stress—for the most part, stress that grows by accumulation, stress that fills the cup until it overflows. Cumulative stress is not simply chronic stress, because chronic stress can remain at the same level indefinitely while cumulative stress *increases*. First responders have that slideshow of worst-case scenarios stored away because they have seen so much. They have responded to calls involving suicide, mass shootings, people burned alive trying to escape flames, babies drowned or suffocated in their sleep—everything you can imagine. They have had people die while they're trying to rescue them. They have had to deal with victims' families and friends and with other victims—those made bereft, suicidal, homeless by the incident—who are often hysterical.

Until all departments have instituted regular mental health checks, the job of emptying the cup, of resolving some of the stored-up trauma memories, is up to the firefighters—yes, the very people who have often done all they could to block those memories rather than deal with them.

I can't stress strongly enough how important it is for you to be on the lookout for the signs of acute stress, burnout, compassion fatigue, and PTSD. Whatever it is, you can help keep it from becoming part of your family unit not only by talking openly about it (which we'll be discussing in depth because it is such an important tool in surviving your relationship), but also by making sure your home is a refuge.

That doesn't mean stifling your own feelings or drastically changing your life. But you can, for instance, make sure your bedroom is a place that promotes restful sleep, as sleep disturbances are often the first sign that something isn't right. A great example I give to firefighters when I'm teaching is to ask, "How many of you have young kids?" Of course, more than half will raise their hands. I then ask them what happens if their child misses a nap or doesn't sleep through the night. They all laugh, because we have all been in the store when our toddler who refused to take their nap falls on the floor and begins screaming. It is the same concept in play with our firefighters, when they go for days without a full night's sleep, and then come home and attempt to complete the "honey do" list without a nap just so they can get up tomorrow and do it all again. Lack of sleep intensifies all the reactions we have talked about.

What will help both of you sleep at stressful times? One of the biggest tips for improving your sleep cycle is a bedtime routine. Do your kids have a nighttime routine? I'm certain they do. And why do you keep this schedule at any cost? Because you want them to go to bed and get a good night's sleep—and you need a break from them, honestly.

Here are some tips to help with that routine. A cool, dark bedroom helps, as does a warm shower before bed. Avoiding both alcohol and large meals for three hours before bedtime is wise for many reasons, as is refraining from caffeine. Quiet music is an option, as is a white noise machine. Some people like the sounds of ocean waves or rainfall. Others prefer the machines that simply make "fan" sounds, the pitch and tone of which can be regulated. You don't need to escape from ambient sounds like loud neighbors, planes overhead, or traffic to have a white noise machine. It also helps to still your thoughts, and the noise you might find annoying at first soon becomes a soothing adjunct to sleep.

There are many more tips to improve your sleep. Search "sleep hygiene" to find a wealth of ideas. The key, though, is that if you want something to change or improve you have to try something new.

It's difficult for many people to ask for help, especially when the problem is emotional or mental. Ongoing stress causes behavioral problems—that's a medical fact, not a judgment. Unfortunately, in careers where bravery is lauded and toughness always applauded, where trainings focus on shutting up and dealing with it, the stigma attached to feeling emotionally unwell can keep firefighters from seeking help.

Here's a little sign you can copy and keep on your refrigerator, so you and your firefighter can get used to looking at it:

IT'S OKAY NOT TO BE OKAY.

I will admit I need help...

...if my coping skills and support system aren't working anymore.

...if I doubt my own coping skills.

...if I lack a healthy support system.

...if I start to feel life isn't worth it anymore.

...if I'm using alcohol or drugs to numb the pain.

...if I no longer have anything I enjoy doing.

...if I do enjoy doing certain things but just don't do them anymore.

...if I just need someone to vent to.

And if I'm not 100% sure about any of these, I will ask for help.

As a significant other, you can't take it for granted that your partner will share things with you, since, after all, they might not even be aware of it themselves. It's easy to overlook just one more drink than usual, or to hide the lying awake at night. And your partner could actually be showing the problem to you. How often and for how long can we resent yet shrug off someone else's behavior until it becomes too harsh to be ignored?

I would say that nine out of ten first responders do not just walk in on a single bad scene and get PTSD. It all depends on that cup.

You could even say most first responders have some degree of PTSD. Cumulative stress is like a cut that starts to fester and get infected. When the first responder ignores it, when they go into denial and take no steps to heal it, to resolve it, it will push them into acute stress.

Still doing nothing? It encodes and then sticks. And it sticks and sticks, hanging on for a month, six months, even years. And then, one day, their cup—already full of perceived demands, full to overflowing—has one more drop added, just one drop, one bad call, one accident...and they snap.

And this is how first responders get in trouble.

This is why self-care is critical. And why getting help isn't an option but a necessity.

Help can be found in many ways and places, including private insurance, employee assistance programs (EAP), the International Association of Firefighters (IAFF), and intensive outpatient programs (IOP). A great asset to the movement of behavioral health in the fire service has been peer support. It has been gratifying to see that, in recent years, more departments have added trained peer supporters who have been schooled to spot the red flags of behavioral problems and reach out to talk things through or offer referrals. Because we are fire families, any of us—whether firefighter or significant other— will need a therapist or clinician who understands our world.

Fire service couples often don't gain insight the way others do. For example, if they go in for regular couples counseling, much time can be lost, simply because that counselor hasn't been trained to know what first responders and their partners are up against.

Finding the right clinician is the most important part to this equation. If you go to an appointment and think, *Wow, I really don't like this therapist*, that's okay. Don't give up; try again until you have a good connection and feel comfortable. I will also add in the *Appendix* a list of questions you can use to interview a therapist on the phone to see if they have experience working with first responders or veterans. Many treatments can help, from traditional talk therapy to cognitive therapy to the Eye Movement Desensitization Reprocessing (EMDR) I talked about in the *Introduction*.

As I said at the very start, I am committed to helping you see that you're not alone. And you can be committed to making sure your firefighter knows that you're there to help *them* feel less alone, that you're their safe harbor. This doesn't mean you can't fight like crazy sometimes, nor that you have to put up with whatever they dish out. It just means you can remain true to yourself and still be part of the solution and not the problem.

Remember, flashbacks to critical incidents and accumulated stress, whether or not they turn into compassion fatigue or PTSD, affect all firefighters. And when they're affected, they don't feel like the strong, capable firefighters portrayed in movies and TV shows. They feel unworthy, weary, and cut off from the rest of the world and their own feelings. They need help: from the department, their crew, trained professionals, peer supporters, and especially those who love them.

Jeff on Responding to 'That' Call

"That" call?

I am thankful that I don't remember all the details anymore: the address, the exact date. Some of those have gone—and I'm glad.

What I do remember is that it was only a few weeks before Christmas. That it involved little kids, and that to this day, it makes no sense to me. Whatever was going on in that house, in that family, was obviously bad.

Like I said, it was a few weeks before Christmas, about four or five years into my professional career. If I remember correctly, it was just another day filled with regular duties and calls. Nothing exceptional.

I don't recall what the call was dispatched as, only that the Sheriff's Office was responding as well. When we arrived, we were directed to the rear entry of the garage. A short flight of stairs led up to the main door. I led the fire and ambulance crews up those stairs. As I reached the landing at the top, one of the deputies, a big man, one whom I respected, burst through the door. All he said was, "They're in there," but I could see on his face something wasn't right—that something was, in fact, very wrong.

I was the first one from Fire through the door. As I crossed the threshold, I yelled back to the rest of the crew, "Don't come in here."

Too late. Many of us were already stacked up in the doorway—chest-to-back, chest-to-back.

What. The. Fuck.

My first thoughts: *This cannot be real...it's a joke, right? Some a-hole staged this, right?* Nope. This was very real. Very *surreal*.

A car parked in the garage had smash marks on the windshield. I must have looked at that car ten times, not wanting to look up again, not wanting to believe what I was really seeing.

Hanging from the open rafters in the garage were a young mother and two small children, maybe three and five years old. Yes, the kids, too...all hanging.

What the hell happened here? And when? How long? Too long. Way too long. No hope. Who did this? Who found them? Now I had a million questions. And the documentation to fill out. I certainly didn't want to say anything in the report that wasn't spot-on. But I couldn't even think right then.

Even as we wrote it up and gave our statements to the Sheriff's Office, arrangements were being made at the station for a CISD (Critical Incident Stress Debriefing). The whole concept was still very new. As we sat and talked openly about what we had just experienced, I did feel some easing of the shock. I don't know how to explain it, but it did feel good just to talk about it.

What we were told next set some of us back a bit. They told us we *had* to go home. I didn't want to. I had nothing there to go to. I had no family to go home to at the time, just an empty house. The message was clear; we didn't have a choice. Whoever had made this decision based it on their own feelings and not ours.

Those of us that weren't going home for whatever reason decided to go out to dinner together. After eating, we ended up at my place, where we drank. A lot.

About a week later, I was out shopping. I hadn't felt any real impacts since the night of the call. I still shook my head at the details; it still didn't make sense to me. But I guess I thought I had already moved past it. And then I got smacked in the face.

Walking toward me were a young mom and her two kids, all about the same age as the people in that garage. These kids were happy and laughing; so was the mom. I felt a knot seize my stomach. I had to sit down. I think I got a little dizzy—I felt weird, anyway. As they moved closer and passed by, I looked away. I waited a few minutes, and my feelings seemed to right themselves. Still... *That's it*, I thought, *I'm outta here. Can't do this today.* I went home, and, yep, I drank. A lot. By myself.

For years, that call affected me. The anxiety I had around Christmas was palpable. Everything from putting up the lights to opening presents on Christmas Day affected me. I recall at some point I hated pretty much everything about Christmas. I was resentful and couldn't enjoy it. I didn't know why, and it wasn't until years later that I finally started to move past it. But it took years. And not having ever addressed it caused some strife around our house during what is supposed to be a joyful time of year.

That call was about twenty-five years ago, a quarter of a century, and it still sneaks back into my brain every now and then. I'm thankful to have learned some things about myself and how to deal with my feelings since then. The right way. Needless to say, I have a wonderful therapist who has obviously played a role in that. I think you know who that is.

SECTION TWO

Being a Partner

CHAPTER FOUR
What You Don't See is What You Get

WHAT WOULD YOUR ANSWER BE if I asked, "Were you surprised by the whole package you ended up with by getting involved with a firefighter?"

Did you realize it could be very tough at times? If you have children, did you expect to be a single parent half the time? Were you prepared for the loneliness, the stressful calls and sleepless nights, the frequent emotional distance?

I'm not here to make you feel bad, and I'm not being negative. I think it's a positive step to consider what we got or are getting into. I learned a lot the hard way—by being unprepared. I want to make it easier for everyone reading this book. I want all of us to feel more whole because we're in something together: all firefighters, all significant others.

As I said, when we met, I was an EMT with a young daughter, and Jeff was a firefighter-paramedic. We knew we wanted to raise a family, so at the beginning of our marriage, we decided that because of his schedule, and since I didn't really have any education or career path at the time, my staying home would be best. And that was the only plan. I didn't have much of a life of my own, as many stay-at-home moms don't. Much of my time, even after our son Kyle joined little Megan, and Jeff got hired by the Long Beach Fire Department, was spent waiting anxiously for my husband to come home. I would plan things for us to do—activities, chores, and outings, all geared toward getting me and the kids out of the house with Jeff, as a family.

This was long before I had a clue about hypervigilance and all the other heavy stuff that comes with the job. Not knowing any better, I would hit my husband with my plans the minute he walked in the door or even earlier, when he called on the way home. Not always, but often, I could guess by his face as he came in, or his tone of voice on the phone, that he wasn't really up for whatever I wanted to do.

Jeff tried hard to be a good sport and do whatever we had planned, even though his heart wasn't in it, but sometimes we'd end up in a fight about something stupid and the day would be ruined. I didn't blame Jeff; I blamed myself. Since I didn't really understand the whole work brain/home brain thing, I truly thought it was about me.

My husband didn't want to hang out with his family. He didn't want to hang out with *me*. I felt shattered. But I'd push it out of my mind until the next time.

Over time, this situation and my thought process worked on my self-esteem and affected our marriage. I felt I had become a weirdly distorted version of myself. I knew it was all connected in some way with how Jeff felt, and I strove to shift my behavior as far as planning for Jeff's days off. Since I had developed the ability to gauge from Jeff's voice even before he arrived at the house what kind of day it would be,

I started a routine to get a better feel for his mood and what kind of day we were in for. I would call Jeff on his way home, not to tell him the plans I hoped for but to hear his voice, to listen for "*that* tone." The tone of his voice told me without words which Jeff was coming home.

The other thing I relied on was asking, "Did you get any sleep last night?" Again, before I knew better, I assumed that if he had slept, we were good to go. What I learned later is that the sleep they get at the station isn't really a restful sleep. It's that waiting for the calls to come in kind of sleep.

All the way up the ranks, it was the same pattern. I was tricked again when my husband was promoted to battalion chief. Since he now didn't go on all the calls, and would sleep all night some shifts, I would be completely thrown off when he came home with that same tone or look. Once the brain is conditioned to respond a certain way in a certain environment, it doesn't stop with a promotion. Jeff continued to sleep in the same pattern with one eye open, waiting, anticipating.

If it was going to be a good day, I got the kids ready to go out or the "honey do" list prepared. If I heard the tone as a level orange alert, I knew all plans must be scrapped and I had to prepare for interaction with the creature who was about to invade our home.

It sounds simple now, but it was grueling. Instead of being able to relax and enjoy our relationship, I was trying to anticipate his every mood and base my own and my children's behavior and plans on that mood. It was not only exhausting—it also created tons of anxiety in both me and the kids.

And the preparation! I wrote in *Chapter One* how we prepared for Jeff's arrival after his shift. It wasn't like any other dad coming home after three or four days away on business. We would have a tactical meeting the day before, when I assigned Megan and Kyle, who were both old enough to help out at this point, cleaning and tidying chores. Then we all rushed around, frantically making sure everything was in its rightful place. I've always been competitive (but you probably figured this out by now, right?), so I always strove to win our little game of "everything in its place" without Jeff pointing out anything that wasn't.

Understanding hypervigilance as you now do, do you think in twenty-three years I've ever won that competition?

If Jeff called while we were dashing around, dusting and vacuuming, and opening and closing drawers, to announce he had been mandatoried and couldn't come home, we all but had a party. "Abort mission!" I'd shout to the kids when I hung up. "Dad has to work tomorrow!" It's not like we didn't want him home; I'd just be so anxious about his mood and what he'd say about things not being clean enough or put away right. As the kids got older, I noticed they grew anxious, too; my daughter even stayed in her room on his first day off.

It bothered me that the kids and I felt like this, but I didn't understand why Jeff acted the way he did. I continued to think it was about me or something I wasn't doing right. Had I known it had nothing to do with me, and that there were things we could do as a family to make this process better, I would have jumped on it. It would have decreased the number of fights we had.

Now that I know what's going on in his brain and body physiologically, I'm not anxious. We have a transition for going from work to home. I no longer hit him with problems, chores, or sudden plans when he walks through the door.

We haven't even touched on what it's like for those of you who have a career. This adds a whole other dimension to the equation. When your firefighter is walking in the door, and you're walking out, it's like a shift change at the station. You need to give a rundown of who's sick, where the kids need to be today, who has a game, and add, "Oh, can you run to the store?"—all of this as you're running out the door. The problem is that the spouse who isn't a firefighter comes home at night and still has to deal with everything there.

When I went back to work, if the kids got sick or they forgot their homework or lunch money, they called me and not their dad. I would have to leave my job to attend to whatever was going on, frustrated and jealous because Jeff got to focus 100 percent on his work while I was the one always making excuses at my own.

Can you see how this would cause so much tension in a relationship? Sure, I had signed up for this, but I wasn't thinking about what was going to happen when I had two kids and a career. Like I always say, being married to a firefighter sounds good in theory, but in practice it's a lot harder.

Life as a (Married) Single Mom

Whose fault was this, anyhow? I didn't blame anyone. Even at my most frustrated, I knew that wasn't the solution. I had known what I was getting into (or so I'd thought), so I knew I'd be on my own a lot. But, as I've said, there's a big gap between theory and practice. And in practice, it was harder and lonelier than I had expected, prepared or not. I was devastated.

Much of the time, my being overwhelmed led to anger and resentment, like when Jeff would come home groaning about how tired he was because he had been up all night. *Oh, don't mind me,* I'd retort silently. *I was just up all night with a sick kid!* While I was busily cleaning up vomit and poop like a good mom, I was thinking jealously of my husband having all sorts of fun, hanging with his buddies at work.

I didn't mean to feel that way, but I couldn't help it sometimes—like when I'd been on the run all day, cleaning, shuttling the kids around, and buying groceries—and then the lord of the manor would come home grumpy, and respond to my saying I was tired with, "Really? What have you got to be tired from?"

Grr. It became an ongoing competition, about who worked harder or was the most overwhelmed. For me, it was as if Jeff never appreciated all I did with cleaning and laundry, shopping and cooking, plus being a full-time parent to the kids and more.

Once I started working, of course, I could throw in fighting over who was going to take the day off when the kids were sick. Going back to school and working changed a lot of things, but I always felt as if he didn't consider my career as important as his.

The bottom line was that I didn't feel valued. I have heard many other significant others complain about these issues, especially stay-at-home moms. It's hard to be happy in a marriage if you feel your contributions to it aren't appreciated or considered equal. When I speak to firefighters, I always remind them that personal relationships are a team sport. No one can be in a relationship all by themselves. We appreciate that our significant others' lives are hard; still, we don't want ours to be dismissed or demeaned.

But I didn't feel resentful every moment. I love my husband, and I would be deeply sad for him when he had to miss one of the kids' games, plays, or presentations of awards they had won. As technology improved and FaceTime came into existence, I could call him from one of Kyle's baseball games, for instance, so he could watch and hear what was going on.

I knew he was missing out on a lot of things he wished he could be there for, but he was missing out on a lot of the challenges of raising children, too. One of the hardest aspects of being on my own so much was having to always play the bad guy and hand out punishments. Sometimes I was so frustrated I would call Jeff and insist, "You need to talk to *your* son!" Jeff would say okay, but then Kyle would take off, with me running after him, holding the phone out on speaker so Jeff could be the one to say, "Knock it off, kid!"

I know, I know—it's not the most effective parenting technique, but when you've run out of tricks, you will try *anything*. This story is hilarious to Jeff and me now because we can look back at our life of ups and downs and see where we could've done things better.

If I had been a genuine single mom, everyone would know who was in charge. But I wasn't, and it wasn't so cut and dried. In fact, it was one of the most difficult aspects of child-rearing. Since I was the most available parent, the kids got used to coming to me for everything—even when their father was home. It was only natural that Jeff wanted to be involved. After all, it was *our* family. And in this case, I was pretty guilty, because Jeff would try to help with something and I'd push him off, saying something like, "No, that's not how we do it," or, "Just let me do it."

I basically set him up in a no-win position. I complained that he wasn't home enough, but when he was there, I'd tell him he wasn't doing something right. And, in case you wondered, I was so used to doing things a certain way, it never occurred to me that Jeff's way wasn't actually wrong but simply wasn't my own.

It's very similar to the way things are done at the station. There is a process the crew does every day and people are assigned to chores. If an overtimer comes in and wants to do it differently, the crew will shut that down. There's one captain in a fire station, which makes it clear every day who is in charge. In our home, we basically have two captains, so it becomes confusing not only to our kids but to both of us as well.

When I finally started back to work part-time, my kids would call all day with stupid questions. Once Kyle called to ask if he could go to a friend's house. "Why are you whispering?" I asked. "And where's your dad?" He answered that his father was "in a mood" and that he didn't want to ask him.

Another time I was in Mississippi, working on a line of duty death, and my kids started fighting over one of the dogs. They decided to add me into their group text. My children are competitive (yes, they're a lot like me and their father), so no one was giving up, and the texting went on for hours. I tried to mediate, but I was having no luck. Reluctantly, I stepped out of the meeting I was in and called the house. Jeff answered in a good mood and asked how my day was going. He was caught off guard when I told him what was going on with the kids—not because they were fighting, as brothers and sisters do, but because he was there in the house and they had texted me, and sucked *me* into their fight, rather than him.

That was when I realized I needed to change my approach. Not only could I not take it all on all the time, but Jeff was their father and wanted to be a good one. Even if his way wasn't my way, it wasn't going to kill the kids. If I stopped getting in the middle, they would adapt to doing things his way.

To be honest, this was easier said than done. I had been in control of so many of our household issues for so long, it was hard to relinquish total control, hard to share it. But—and this is my lesson to you—I discovered that once I did share responsibilities with my husband, it made my life easier. Equally important, it allowed Jeff and the kids to build their own relationship without having me in the middle. And, finally, it brought Jeff and me closer because I was letting him into the circle of trust.

Regaining My Independence

When I was staying home with the kids, my discomfort wasn't just about feeling hassled and underappreciated. It was also that I didn't feel I was contributing enough to the family. I couldn't help but feel guilty about the long hours Jeff was working to support us and allow me to be a stay-at-home mom; in fact, that was one of the reasons I held back so much in the beginning. I felt I should be grateful and not complain. But that lack of communication was what built up resentment in me. I was already taking a couple of classes here and there, before Kyle was born; it was pretty easy, because Megan was seven and there was a neighbor girl who babysat. I never had to count on Jeff's being there in order to go out for a while, and I always had a backup plan for day care. I was pregnant with Kyle when I was getting my BS and had him a few months before I graduated.

It was harder when I went back for my master's degree. I had to be creative again, because I couldn't depend on Jeff being home (especially during fire season) to take care of the kids. I found an evening program and would feed and bathe both children, so all the babysitter had to do was put them to bed. And I felt comfortable because, at eight, Megan knew her brother's schedule. As Kyle got older, the challenge was finding a way to balance time with him and Megan and still get my homework done. I'd stay up late writing papers, or take my laptop into Kyle's room and keep him company while he played video games.

One of the hardest things about going back to school was that now my husband and I had something new to be competitive about. Jeff had always wanted to get his education, but working and supporting us was the priority at the time, so this became a sore spot and the root of many arguments. Don't get me wrong—he was my biggest supporter, but it was hard for him to have to wait to get his own degree.

When he did finally get his BS from Long Beach State University, it was a great day for both of us. One of the big things we learned as a fire family: timing is everything when goals are being met. Sometimes the plan had to be one goal at a time. Jeff worked on his career and promotion and I went to school. Once I was done with school, he went. It was a plan we agreed to, but again, "theory versus practice."

As I said in the beginning of this book, I thought I wanted to be a teacher at first, but substitute teaching put an end to that. It just wasn't for me. My academic counselor was the one who suggested I'd be good at counseling, so I switched paths to get my MS in counseling. And I loved it! I was hooked. I still had to be cautious about the time of my classes and who would pick up the kids from school, if Jeff was at work or out on a fire assignment. Of course, as they got older, I didn't have to worry about having someone there to take care of them. Then again, that was replaced by having to sort out their frequent fights.

Now I had my daughter calling me frequently, complaining about her bratty brother. It was typical sibling rivalry, with Megan starting off with "He did *this!*" and Kyle going on to "Well, she said *that!*" And as if my working toward a degree and dealing with two bickering kids weren't enough, Jeff got promoted twice while I was in school. That meant both of us were studying or under the gun at the same time.

Surprise: the house buzzed with big-time increased tension. Somehow, we got through this and figured out we all had to be patient with one another and remember the bigger goal. In our case, this was that our continuing education and seeking higher qualifications would improve our quality of life in every way. The *why* is so much more important than the *what*. We just had to keep reminding ourselves to take our hyperfocused blinders off and look at the big picture.

I said in the beginning that part of the reason I went back to school was to converse with adults, and go pee by myself—and even though it wasn't the main reason I loved school and kept going, it was definitely rewarding to have an identity besides wife and mom (and, yes, to pee alone). There is nothing I love like being a mother, and my husband is amazing, but I felt as if I were missing some piece of myself.

School also opened a world of socializing outside the fire service that continues to affect us today. I made girlfriends to hang out with, and we started getting together with other couples more often. Even now, most of our friends came from either my schooling or our kids' sporting events.

And have I mentioned that starting school was a huge boost to my self-esteem? I didn't just feel like a more competent and more interesting person—I knew I was one!

How What I Learned in School Saved My Marriage

Studying for my master's in marriage and family therapy made me aware of how little I knew about human behavior. Many things started to fall into place about marriage and communication.

My poor husband played the guinea pig for my assignments, and he was incredibly sweet about it. As I said, even when we fought, he tried to be as supportive of my career as possible. So, when I would come home from class and tell him I had to videotape myself doing this or that type of therapy, his reply was always the same: "What person am I playing for this one?" Jeff always says he got a master's with me, and I honestly believe he did. He learned, along with me, as I practiced the new communication skills I would need for my future clients. It helped us tremendously in the long run. Don't get me wrong—we still fight and struggle like every couple, but we have at least added a few more tools that help us work through some of it.

I started seeing the patterns we had fallen into in our relationship. Like many people who feel they should be grateful and never moan, or who hold everything in because they decide it's just not worth fighting over, I would make passive-aggressive statements to get my digs in, and then, when we did fight, I would haul out everything I had previously decided not to mention and unload it all. It was like a bomb dropping. Remember, when you hold things in, whether they're traumatic incidents or resentments, they don't go away but lie dormant, waiting for the first opportunity to rear their ugly heads.

As I see it, there are three stages to a relationship, and not every relationship survives them. The beginning is sweetness and light, and never wanting to make waves or cause conflict. Then comes the angry and continuously annoyed phase.

In this phase, I often went from one extreme to another, from keeping my mouth shut to saying whatever was on my mind. This middle phase was the one in which our marriage wasn't the best. If you have been through this phase, or if you're still going through it, you know how draining it is. We seemed to argue about everything—literally everything—yet we weren't able to sit down and have an adult conversation about it. We were both on the offensive and angry at each other, while also being defensive and unwilling to hear what the other person thought and felt, because we were too busy defending ourselves and our grievances.

I'm in the third and final phase now. This is the stage where you've adjusted to the pressures, worked out your differences, and learned to communicate. A lot of this is because much of the stress of parenting is gone, now that the kids are adults with their own lives. I'm eyeball-deep in my own career now, too.

Most things don't bother me the way they used to. Sure, I still miss Jeff when he's at work, but I no longer complain as much about his overtime work or fire assignments. When he leaves, I see it as a chance to spend more time with friends or have some me time.

When he comes home in a bad mood now, I get it. I don't take it personally. I've also developed enough self-esteem to call him out. I'll ask if he's mad at me for any reason. If he says no, I'll tell him, "If you're in a bad mood from work, I understand, but please go and do something to decompress so you won't take it out on me." We have stopped trying to be mind readers. We just come right out and ask the questions we'd like answers to. If Jeff had a bad call, I'll ask if he wants to talk about it. Sometimes he does, sometimes he doesn't, and I'm fine with either.

We don't snip at each other or fight the way we used to. Why? Because we have worked on not doing that. Jeff has said it's not that the hypervigilance went away—he still has it—but that now he makes better choices about how he lets it out. He tells me that my leaving the damned toaster out still drives him crazy, but now he takes a breath and puts it away. He makes a conscious decision that it's not the toast or me but his work brain, still going. I still call in the morning, when he's at work, to see if he slept last night or just gauge his mood—I don't think I'll ever break that habit—and now we ask each other, "What does your day look like? Is there anything I can do to help? Do you need me to do something?" This way, we've taken out the guesswork, and we can tell each other how we feel and what we need.

It's not that all of our problems went away, or that we never fight and we're perfect. The stressors of the fire life are still there; they didn't disappear. However, with our maturity, doing it all wrong, not knowing any better, and almost demolishing our marriage, we have learned a few things. I really do believe that once you truly understand how far-reaching the ripple can go from this career, you will change your perspective and view the stressors differently, thus handling them in more appropriate ways.

Now that Jeff is getting to the end of his career, our focus has to shift again. The fire life is always about being able to adapt to and evolve with the job's demanding lifestyle. It's not all bad, not at all, but

I had preconceived ideas of what a marriage was *supposed* be, and they were based on a regular marriage, a sort of nine-to-five, five-days-a-week marriage. Those rules don't fit or apply 100 percent to any fire relationship.

And that's why this book is so important to me and why I speak as often as I can to firefighters and their significant others. We all need what I'm sitting here and working on putting into words: our own rule book that's exclusive to us, to fire families large and small, young and old.

I have a lot to say about communication. I'll offer exercises to help in talking through your relationship problems, as well as some insights from my children on how being in a fire family affects kids. But first—because I have never been in my marriage all by myself— I want to give you Jeff's side of the story. While I was going through all these challenges and changes, he was my partner, both in frustration and, later, in growing and healing. I think the frustrations he had during that tough time in our relationship will help you understand how your own firefighter often feels.

Jeff Tells Why Your Different Worlds Must Come Together or You Grow Apart

The anticipation, for me, when I was on my way back home, was often cruel during those earlier days. I couldn't get there fast enough, and then...and then I'd sometimes wish I were anyplace else.

Take being at fire camp, for instance. The daily grind of an incident gradually wears you out. The first part of the assignment, it's nonstop high adrenaline: planning and directing the battle against the fire, evaluating and making progress checks. It's a special kind of wearing down, though, because the physical demands and mental engagement are fulfilling. You see the results of your work making progress on the fire. It's measurable: the percentage of containment goes up and the release of resources begins.

Strangely, perhaps, to a non-fire person, anxiety starts to build as this part of the process progresses. The thrill of the fight is over and now the work—by all means still a must—turns a bit tedious. We can see the light at the end of the tunnel, and we all want to move toward it. Rapidly. So, we're super-antsy, thinking, *Whoa, get to go home soon! But when? Tomorrow, day after? How long are they gonna keep us here? This fire is out, over, done. I want to go home!*

Every firefighter on the scene wants the same thing, and sometimes you want it so bad you might make the mistake of telling your family, "We're outta here tomorrow!" Don't do it. Just don't. Never say anything about being out until you are on the road. Your family's anticipation is as strong as your own, and if it gets deflated quickly, it brings disappointment and even hostility.

How about it, significant others? Has that happened to you? If it did, I'll bet you were quite pissed off, even if it was only a one-day delay.

Even when you know it's just one day, you still have to wait. You're on the demobilization list, but you have to wait until the next day and fill out the demob sheet before you can get out.

Finally, you're on the road home, but you're not headed straight home. You can't drive fast enough to get back to your department to unpack the vehicle/fire truck you took, and then finally leave for home; when it's me driving home from Long Beach, where I dropped off my truck and equipment, there's always another hour or two on the road, depending on the traffic. And I was, and am, always eager. Then there's that fantastic feeling of making the final turn into the driveway and—ah, I'm finally here!

So, I would walk in the door, rush in, eager to be back with my adoring family and...it would start. "Why didn't you tell me the whatchamacallit was broken?" "How could you forget to pay the electric bill?" "You need to help Megan with her homework while I run to the store and get something for dinner!"

What I'm thinking by then is, WTF? *This is what I rushed home to?*

Here's some more advice to any firefighter reading this: *shut your mouth.* Zip it, my friend. Why? Because you alone have to deal with the reality that your family's life went on without you when you weren't there.

Don't get me wrong. I made this mistake myself. I can be a slow learner. So that's why the anticipation is hard. If you're like me, you eat up that road on the way because you just want to get there, sit back on the couch, relax, and maybe drink a beer. But your family? They might have other plans.

Your family has been doing their thing while you've been off doing yours. And now these two different worlds have come together. I almost always longed for this change of pace and scenery, something different from the last two to three weeks. And much of the time, that something different would be my own living room, at least at first. I never drove home without wanting to disengage completely, to spend time chilling with my wife. I always thought about how happy the whole family would be to see me. Yet sometimes, I knew that wasn't gonna happen. Sure, it sucked. But it couldn't always be just your way.

One time, I got up several hours early and drove literally all day to get to an event that I wasn't expected to be at. As I got closer, I was thinking how cool this would be, how happy they'd be when I got there. Just as I was walking up to where I could spot Mynda, I got a text from her relating something that was happening at that moment. I texted back that, Yeah, I saw it, too. When I got to where she was, she had a second of confusion then gave me the cold shoulder! No "OMG, I'm so glad you're here." No warm embrace. Nah, all I got was, "What the hell are you doing here?"

I turned pale and started to sweat, a lump in my throat. Yeah, that sure went over well. All the anticipation and joy I had been feeling got flushed straight down the toilet. *Great*, I thought, *just fucking great*. The fun dinner I had been thinking about on the drive? Great, nobody wanted to go. All I could say was, "Okay, see you all at home." And *that* drive was too short. The moral of this story is that sometimes the surprise is overwhelming and not really wanted. When you blast into town unexpectedly, it doesn't always work out so well.

(Mynda: I remember that day clearly. It wasn't that we didn't want Jeff there or were angry that he had surprised us. It was just that I had my mental process, the one I went through before Jeff came home so I knew what we would be getting. My immediate reaction when he popped up was, *Why is he here? Did something happen? Doesn't he trust me? How did he get here so fast? Wasn't he just on a fire?* It took just a minute for me to switch my brain to, *Hey, you're home!* But by then it was too late.)

One of the things that most attracted me to Mynda was her drive. When we first met, neither of us was completely happy with where we were, personally or professionally. We both wanted more. As our relationship grew, I realized that Mynda was someone who wouldn't give up on much, if anything. And that strengthened the attraction.

When she went back to school, it changed. I felt like all I did was work while she got to stay home and also get an education. I was jealous and frustrated. She was getting something I wanted, something I felt I deserved and that I knew I needed for my job in order to advance through the ranks. I might have been going through the motions of support, but I was fooling only myself. And I don't know exactly what happened—something Mynda said or did, I'm sure—that forced me to get my head out of my ass and see the bigger picture. But I finally did. I started doing a lot more to try and make up for it, but, while she showed me some appreciation, I know my actions and attitude prior to my snapping out of it were engraved in her mind.

As Mynda continued getting more degrees than a thermometer, I worked hard at taking this new approach. I was as supportive as I could be, recognizing that my jealousy was the problem and that I had to get over it. By the time she entered the doctoral program, I was okay. Having accomplished my own educational goals helped. And then I realized, *Wow, I'm going to be married to a doctor!* The workload couldn't be easy, and I knew I absolutely had to be supportive. I wasn't even jealous now, because I knew there was no way I would be attempting this level of education. I'm just not wired that way.

As the months crept by, Mynda met some resistance both inside and outside the program, but it only increased her drive and made her want it more, wanted it to be even better. She became so focused on being successful that I could hardly believe how concentrated she was. On the day of her dissertation defense, I must have looked like a kid in a candy store. I know I was beaming, thrilled, so proud of her. When I heard the board's comments, it really sank in how amazing the journey and struggle had been for her, for us. Can you imagine the relief I felt that I had caught myself in time and hadn't spoiled it for her?

As I have been sitting and writing this, putting my words into this book, her book, it dawned on me that the education I had been searching for, I got. It was a different form of learning, both before and after I got my sheepskin, because I learned so much through practical experience. The job itself, even more than that degree I had coveted for so long, was my education. The job has given me an education.

And what I learned from all this and want to share with you is that you must accept that your relationship cannot be a competition. As my wife so perfectly puts it, it's a team sport, an experience for both of you. There may be imbalances as far as who accomplishes what and when, but it will all work out if you have a plan, if you're both on the same page and working on the same mission. As to how to get there, talking about it is the key. *Communication.* It comes up in every AAR (after action review). Why wouldn't it come up in a marriage? And I don't know anyone better than Dr. Ohs for sharing with you the communication skills that will make your relationship a success, as they did ours.

SECTION THREE

Being a Family

CHAPTER FIVE

Fire World Parenting, Fire World Kids

C HILDREN LEARN FROM THEIR PARENTS, but we parents also learn from our kids. As well as I know them, even I learned a few things from what Megan and Kyle have related about their feelings growing up. Fire world kids know they exist in a different sphere from their friends, even if they're not always sure why. Since Jeff and I were working it all out, Megan and Kyle had to come along for the ride and work out much for themselves as well.

In retrospect, I wish I had known then what I know now—and it's why I've written this book for you, to help you avoid some of the pain and pitfalls we all had to get through to get to where we are now.

As you will see from what my children wrote, they turned out very well—sometimes because of us, and sometimes in spite of us. Both Jeff and I are proud of them and happy in turn that they are so proud to belong to a fire family. We all got through it and emerged closer and stronger. You can do it, too.

Part One: Megan

The very first memory I have of my dad is pretty funny. I was five or six years old, and he was picking up my mom for a date. I was an introverted little girl, feeling shy when faced with this strange man sitting in the small living room of our duplex while my mother was in the bathroom getting ready—and then he called me over and told me to go pinch my mom's butt. I thought this was hilarious. Of course, I obliged. I snuck into the bathroom, pinched her butt, and ran out laughing. That made me like Jeff right from the start. Oh, what a smooth icebreaker he was!

You may be wondering what this has do with growing up in a fire family, but—before the not-so-fun, nitty-gritty parts, the parts about calling my dad "the Funsucker" and not having him around much of the time—I want to take it back to the beginning, to the time he and my mom got together, a time when I needed him the most, and how it changed my life forever.

At the time Jeff showed up, the man who was currently occupying the role of "Dad" was a deadbeat who kind of all-around sucked. Even though he and my mom had just started dating, Jeff immediately stepped into the part, attending my sporting events and even taking me to school. I saw my biological dad differently, once I had someone to compare him to. Not surprisingly, I stopped visiting him by the age of ten, even before Jeff adopted me. My point here is about the qualities possessed by firefighters and how they make great parents in spite of the stress and challenges.

I chalk up my ability to adapt to growing up in a fire family. I had to adapt constantly to the different environments within my house: mom environment, dad environment, and mom-dad environment.

"Mom environment" was when my dad was gone twenty-four or seventy-two hours, or even longer when he was on a fire. "Dad environment" was when just my dad was at home, and "mom-dad environment" was when everyone was home. Now, dad environment was the least common and the shortest since first my mom stayed at home and then was at school only part-time. When I was a teenager and my mother was working, the dad environment was more frequent.

Since my dad's work schedule was twenty-four hours on and twenty-four hours off, I had to constantly adapt, from one day to the next, to different environments. It's always your house and your parents, but it's like stepping into a different house each time.

Like my mom, I remember my dad's time in the academy being hard on us all. I definitely felt the tension and stress. However, after Jeff had been at the department for some time and I was sixteen, I got to go on my first twenty-four-hour ride-out, which changed everything for me.

At the time, my dad worked at Station 10, the busiest station in Long Beach. One of the calls we went on involved a drive-by shooting. It was so hectic! At one point, while tending to the victim, my dad handed me a saline bag that was hooked up to the guy and said, "Hold this up." That was the coolest thing ever, helping on an actual call, and an epic adrenaline rush. The calls ranged from serious to BS throughout the day, each one different. In that single twenty-four-hour shift, we ran twenty-six calls—or, more accurately, *they* did. I was so exhausted, my dad couldn't even wake me for the last two calls.

We lived in Highland, California, at the time, which meant that when "we" got off that morning, there was still about an hour's drive to look forward to. My dad drove. Me? I was instantly asleep and remained KO'd the entire ride home. I woke up just long enough when we got home to tell my mom everything that had happened.

I gained a new appreciation for my dad that day, and that was just a twenty-four-hour shift. There were many times he worked at that station three times as many hours. I don't know how he did it, but after that, I understood why he would come home exhausted or in a "mood."

What I didn't understand until I started working in EMS myself was why he didn't go straight to sleep when he got home like I had. When my dad came home, especially after working seventy-two hours, and refused to rest, it created a lot of tension.

My routine involved "testing the waters," coming out of my cave of a room to gauge what kind of mood he was in. If he was cheerful and immediately said hi to me, I relaxed. On the flip side, if I came out and he had *that look* in his eyes and didn't say anything, that was my cue to retreat. I recognized that look. It told me that any mistake I made—even failing to immediately do what he asked or not putting a dish in the dishwasher the way he wanted—would be like WWIII. I just didn't want to deal with it, so I became the ultimate conflict avoider, as opposed to trying to talk to my dad in a healthy manner.

I suspected it wouldn't go anywhere, so I avoided trying to talk it out. Part of my dad's "Funsucker" persona was when he was in these moods and wouldn't do anything to decompress or spend some time alone; he would always remain in the living room, making everyone else experience his "awesome" mood. Then when I *would* want to hang out with him and the family, he would be too busy decompressing or dealing with the awful sights he had seen in the best way that he could. Being a kid, I just thought he was being hard on me, which didn't make me much fun to deal with, either.

As time went on, I got better at adapting to each new schedule change of my dad being home or away. As an adult, after working in EMS and being in school for a master's in social work, I understood what was going on with my dad. I know he saw many traumatic things and had to deal with them in his own way. And instead of having the space in which to sort it out, he had to come home and be expected to immediately switch into home brain.

I learned later how it felt to work a twelve-hour shift in the emergency room as an ER-tech on an extremely busy day, with repeated adrenaline spikes that called for quickly getting a patient on a gurney and hooked up to the machines that would monitor the patient's blood pressure, pulse, and heart rate, while making sure I was performing CPR correctly. After twelve exhausting hours, coming home and trying to unwind is hard. I remember coming home from work on those days and going straight to my room without talking to anyone. This continued when I started working with psychiatric patients in that same ER, having to be constantly on guard because many of them were unpredictable and aggressive, and I had to be prepared to avoid getting injured. Being on alert for hours is mentally exhausting. And you don't even realize how exhausting it is until you get home. I realize now that my dad would try his best to hang out with us and do family things, but his inability to switch to home brain got in the way of us having fun together on many occasions.

I live in Las Vegas with my significant other, having moved here from California about a year ago. At the time, I was working in an ER with psychiatric patients, and we were in a long-distance relationship—something that requires a lot of effort, because the distance is an added strain. I was often working overtime, and there was a period when neither he nor I thought we were going to make it. One factor I was struggling with, and that he didn't like, was that I didn't want to talk on the phone after work. He wanted to hear my voice, which wasn't an unrealistic request, but on my end, after those twelve hours of hypervigilance, I didn't have it in me to talk on the phone to anyone. And, no, *I couldn't even pick up the phone and talk to my boyfriend?* I didn't have the mental capacity at that point. When I did try to talk to him, it went one of two ways: I would either have nothing to say and respond like a caveman, or I would be irritable and pick at him. Obviously, there is a happy ending to this story, but I gained a new respect for what my dad went through every day for decades and still continues to deal with.

I work in a psychiatric hospital here in Vegas. The number one difference, obviously, is that I am now living with my significant other. But equally important, I became more flexible and changed, because he let me have it! He told me he didn't like the lack of communication and that he felt he was making an effort and I wasn't. So, I learned to compromise and communicate more effectively with my partner. I learned, as my mom did way back when, that you have to make some compromises, admit when you are wrong, and always be open to communicating. Get it out, because if you don't you are just a ticking time bomb.

My hope is that you and your firefighter, if you have been keeping things from your children, will now talk openly with them about the struggles of being a firefighter and why their mom or dad sometimes acts the way that they do. If you explain this to your kids early on, they will be more understanding of their firefighter parent. I wish I had been told more as a kid, because I would have understood what my dad went through and what we could all do to get along better. I think it would have also helped me realize it wasn't me (all the time) that he was mad or upset with.

We got through it all because my parents worked hard at it. Yes, there were times when my dad couldn't be there, but I can honestly look back and say he was always there when it was possible. When he couldn't come to events, I accepted that he had to work. I may have been biased, because my biological father failed me, but the fact that Jeff made it to every event on every single one of his days off was amazing. And while he could never be the head coach of any team I played on, he somehow managed to be the assistant coach of most of them, because that's the type of father and person he is.

I always thought my dad being a firefighter was the coolest thing in the entire world. I knew he was different from other fathers and that he would never be home every night at five o'clock, but I honestly didn't care. And he has done it for so long, it's all I know. Before I met my boyfriend, I actually worried about being with a guy who came home every night, afraid I would get sick of him!

The fire family is something I will always love being a part of. Fire service truly is a family, and it's hard to explain the bond, the brotherhood, until you have been at a firehouse. I always admired their bond, but I didn't quite understand it until I starting working in EMS, which is much the same, just on a smaller level. I understood why my own family members have a foul sense of humor, a tendency toward sarcasm, and a smart-ass mouth. Between EMS and working in the ER, I realized that firefighters forge bonds because of all the crap they see on a daily basis. When you see horrifying things you will never forget, you bond—and you all develop the same twisted sense of humor. I have laughed so hard with EMS and ER friends that my stomach hurt. I will never forget the day a six-month-old baby was brought, unresponsive, into the ER, or the mother's screams echoing throughout the whole department when her child couldn't be revived. My dad experienced trauma like this all the time when I was growing up, even though I didn't know about it at the time. It affected him to his core, and I now know that what I chalked up then as "in a mood" was my dad dealing with all that while he was also trying to adapt from one environment to the other and trying not to let us down. All those years when I was trying to adapt to his coming home and leaving, I didn't realize he was doing the same.

Not everyone is as fortunate as my dad, knowing exactly what they want to do for the rest of their life. He was made for this job, that he truly loves it, and that he cares about people on a level I have not seen elsewhere.

I believe I have finally found my own niche, but it took some time. First, I wanted to work for law enforcement and do crime scene investigation. Discouraged at how hard it was to get into the field, I decided to go the medical route. I went to college to be a physician's assistant, which is when I became an EMT in the emergency room for clinical experience, and worked with psychiatric patients in the ER as well. I liked it, but I knew that being a physician's assistant wasn't something I wanted to do for the rest of my life. I had a four-year degree and was back at square one—not completely, because now I definitely wanted to work with first responders, law enforcement, or EMS. I just wasn't sure in what way.

The desire to work with first responders was because of my dad and because I was so used to dealing with and being around a certain kind of people. I don't want to be a firefighter (and my brother is filling that space). My ultimate goal remains going into law enforcement, but in the meantime, I started working on a master's degree in social work. If I don't get hired with a department, I will finish my degree. I don't want to do typical social work, but concentrate on what my mom does. While I am still trying to find my path, I know my parents have been the major influence of my career choice. They love what they do and are successful, so I can only hope to be just like them.

Part Two: Kyle

I always knew what my dad did. I never even wondered; I just always knew. I spent most of my childhood in a fire station, because my dad worked so much. I had a lot of toys that were fire-related, and I even had costumes, junior fireman getups that made me feel even more a part of my dad's life.

The fire service has always been the life I've known, and it's what I honestly believe I was made for. I learned quickly as I was growing up that you either called people by their rank or last name. To me, they weren't a bunch of firefighters—they were my family. I actually saw them more often than I ever saw my extended family.

I can't even remember the first time I visited a fire station to see my dad, because I remember being a kid as always being there. I spent a lot of major holidays and weekends at the station, not just because I wanted to be around my dad but because I was addicted to being there. It was almost as if I not only wanted to be there, but had to be.

Once I started playing sports and having events in my life, I wasn't at the station as much. The best part was that my dad was able to make trades or take days off, so he got to see me play at a lot of them. But even when he couldn't be there, I understood why he wasn't. It's not like he was busy trying to sell a house or pushing papers—he was saving people's lives, doing something that always seemed a lot bigger than some stupid baseball game. While I missed his being around more, I never questioned it. I was proud of what he did and of his commitment.

Since you are reading this, I'm pretty sure you know enough about firefighters to know that we are not the quietest or most discreet people. It was obvious when my parents were yelling, when they were fighting, or when they'd had a fight and were avoiding each other, like if it was my dad's only day off in two weeks and he was on the opposite side of the house not talking to my mom. I don't remember being upset by it; to me, it was just the way my folks were. As I grew older and my own life got busier, the tensions and disagreements stopped not only because I was gone but because my parents had gotten better at working it out.

I was still young when my mom went back to school the first time. When she went for her PhD I was older, so I can clearly remember being amazed that she was doing it. I realized this was far from an easy task. I remember doing my homework with her as she did hers, and even trying to help her when she made PowerPoints for her class, since she used to always help me with mine.

A lot of the kids I grew up around did not have family in a first responder field. Most had stay-at-home moms and dads who worked regular jobs. It didn't matter to me. I was aware that their lives weren't like ours, but everyone's life is different from each other's, so I didn't pay attention to it. But I see now that many of those kids struggled in their early adulthoods because they didn't have to grow up as quickly as I did.

My sister and I didn't have a good relationship when I was young. Megan and I are eight years apart, so she thought she was my mom sometimes, or believed my mom was too easy on me since I was the baby. She tried to be as strict with me as my parents were with her, which made me dislike her. We fought a lot, because of that. As we both grew up, our relationship changed. It's excellent, now; we get along well and talk like normal siblings. It's not easy to stay in touch since we're both so busy. It's not the normal busy. Living in Las Vegas, working in a psychiatric hospital, going for her master's degree, and me being a firefighter, trying to fit in as much training and work experience as I can get, make it much more difficult to find time to email or pick up a phone than it would be for a brother and sister who grew up in a normal family and made different career choices.

As I said, I somehow always knew I'd choose the fire life for my own. I always knew my dad's job was dangerous, but it never affected me when I was younger. The mortality factor really hit when I entered the field. The more close (near-death) calls I went on, the more and more it put that into perspective.

But the day it really hit home and brought me to my knees was June 25, 2018, when my dad called at 6:30 a.m. and told my mom, who then came into my room to tell me, that Long Beach Fire Captain Dave Rosa had been killed on duty. A lot of the men who raised me in the station are like my second dads or uncles. They are truly family. To hear that one of them had died while serving—especially Dave, a man who had taught me vital things about this job, and allowed me to do things at the station and helped mold me to become who I am today—was by far the hardest and worst thing I have experienced in my life so far. And it really drove home for me that I had been born into this life and had grown up to choose it for myself—and that knowing the risks and the challenges didn't change how I felt about the fire world, that it was my world and I wanted to be nowhere else.

As for my dad, it has always been difficult when he comes home. Being tired and mentally drained is a struggle, and I understand that now more than I possibly could have before. I used to make a point of staying out of his way, but now I make fun of him since he's "just" a battalion chief and not running calls all night like he used to. So, in my mind, he doesn't have an excuse to be an ass. I'm laughing as I write this, because that's part of being a firefighter, too. I inherited my dad's irreverent sense of humor, and that's also a nice legacy.

Just a Few Words from Jeff

And here we are, a first responder legacy family. We made it, and we're all still on speaking terms. As Mynda said, we are proud parents personified. If you have kids of your own, you know there is nothing that matches the sense of wonder that comes from molding children into terrific adults—even if they don't always shower their father with respect and applause every time he tells them something.

But great as it is, my pride in Megan and Kyle is more than equaled by what they have written about me here. It makes me feel something I don't often feel, and I am truly humbled. It means so much to me that my kids saw past my so frequently grumpy, hypervigilant exterior to the loving father beneath. And the fact that both have chosen to be first responders, that they decided they wanted to be like their mom and dad? If nothing else amazing happens to me in my life—and it will, because look at the family I've got!—the joy of that will have made everything worthwhile.

I hope one day you will be able to look at your own family and, even if you can't say it now, say the same. Just remember, you need patience, flexibility, and the determination to make your relationship work.

Mynda and I have lived all the exercises and suggestions she makes. And the result? As I said, here we are all together, and what could be better than that?

I love my family. Always have, always will. I know I wasn't there all the time, and I know I didn't act the way I could have all the time, but I wouldn't change what we did, how we did it, and how we lived. It has made us who we are. And we are strong.

I'm so proud of my family. They have all become what they wanted. They impress me so much. Overcoming my shortfalls and being able to understand and adapt to them, yet all the way pursuing their dreams? Our kids with their careers, our family coming together in this book to share our experiences with you?

Amazing.

While my family and I struggled sometimes with our dynamic, we never lost our faith in each other. I wish the same for you.

SECTION FOUR

*Talk Openly Now So You Don't
Talk about Divorce Later*

CHAPTER SIX
Identify Major Challenges, Own Your Responsibility

T IMES HAVE CHANGED, and few people nowadays expect their partner to take care of everything at home—no one expects their significant other to be the one who is totally in charge of paying bills, dropping clothes at the dry cleaner, or being solely in charge of the kids. But because firefighter relationships are a breed apart, significant others need to perfect the balance between independence and dependence. This balance is individual: what works for one couple might not work for another, and the balance can change from time to time within a relationship—but creating and adjusting it isn't the same as it is for other couples.

We all need to learn to take care of things on our own. This is true of people in general, but it's true of fire service significant others in particular because their partner is unable to help out at home, much of the time, due to the demands of their chosen career. When I say "on our own," I don't mean literally being Superman or Supermom.

I mean being in charge and capable. I am telling you about this so that if and when something breaks down—whether it is backed-up plumbing, a broken sprinkler, or a stuck garage door—you won't do what I did early in my marriage, which was, as you have probably guessed, to call Jeff at work and ask plaintively, "What should I do?"

Firefighters are fixers, so, naturally, Jeff would get angry or irritated that something had gone wrong on my watch, when he wasn't there to fix it. We would get into those phone conversations with dead silences in between tense sentences. He would ask (okay, a reasonable question, I admit), "What do you want me to do about it when I'm working?"

My reaction was not an unusual one, when faced with that kind of question. Through gritted teeth, I'd say tightly, "Never mind," while silently vowing not to call him again.

This was definitely not a solution, because it meant Jeff would come home from work and be met with crisis conditions, like entering a devastated combat zone rather than Home Sweet Home. When slapped with a huge list of stuff needing to be fixed or resolved, the first thing out of his mouth would be "Mynda, *why didn't you tell me?*" And so, there we would be, on the road to nowhere.

I finally worked it out and found my own middle ground, either relying on male friends or paying someone to come and help. I can no longer imagine going through life without a reliable handyman.

I always keep Jeff in the loop, now, so he's never walking in the door unaware. And there are some things I genuinely want his help and only his help with, because they involve mutual decisions. But these days it's pretty automatic for me to put on my Big Girl shoes and handle most things on my own.

If I sound impressively in-control, let me assure you that I wasn't always Big Girl enough to have a real grip on the situation. Like the time when the kids were little and we came home from doing errands to find that one of the dogs had chewed a huge hole in the water heater. When I called Jeff and told him, he asked where I was. I replied that the kids and I were standing in front of the water heater in the garage. I even said, "Listen, you can hear it."

That sure got his heart thudding. He told me to call 911 right away to get immediate help—and to get the hell out of the garage. That's how I learned not only that gas wasn't a great thing to inhale, but that there was that other small issue of its ability to burst into flames and cause explosions.

It didn't take long before I figured out that Jeff wasn't going to be able to ride in on his white stallion to save me every time something went wrong. If you are going to be a fire spouse long term, you need to do that: learn what you can do on your own and how to handle any situation that might come up—not by doing it all alone, but by being prepared and knowing who to call.

First, you need some guys with time on their hands and a love of being Mr. Fixit. Then you need a list of paid rescuers for when all else fails—not just emergency numbers for gas or water leaks, but a reliable plumber, roofer, cleaning service, and handyman.

You also need a support circle, so you aren't literally trying to handle everything alone and keep your sanity, too. This can be family, friends, or your fire family. When Jeff and I were first married, we didn't have family nearby that I could lean on to babysit, fix things, or just keep me company when Jeff was gone on long assignments. Being young, I didn't want to burden anyone with my problems, and, being a stay-at-home mom, I didn't have a lot of friends to rely on. I believed I could do everything on my own, and I didn't want to be a burden on others. But none of us can do that. And that's not what being independent is about, anyhow. Being independent means making decisions without having to call and run every single decision past your significant other—it doesn't mean trying to handle everything totally alone.

I want to stress that you will need help and that it's okay. You don't need to prove anything. You are not in a relationship with a "regular" person, so you need to go with the flow. When I got married, I believed any help I might need would come from my spouse. Having that expectation was a straight, short path to disappointment. I couldn't think outside the box in regard to my circle of trust, and what I got in return for that were doubt, depression, and loneliness.

Now, you might already have a support circle set up. If you do, that's awesome. If you don't, doing whatever is necessary to have one is a critical step for both your own sanity and the longevity of your relationship.

One reason I went back to school is that I knew much of my unhappiness stemmed from needing more out of my life than what I had. Another reason was that I sensed I had to do something for myself, by myself, in order to develop my independence and my circle of support. I couldn't have put it into words at the time, but gradually it sank in that I could not rely on Jeff for the exact type of support I had envisioned before we met. When I tried to, when I depended on him to do something, or was waiting for him to come home so I could have a little free time for myself, and then he either got an overtime or was mandatoried, I was disappointed.

My disappointment would feed my resentment, which flourished. It's a vicious circle.

I know this happens to you, too. I know it because when I lead a class for significant others, I always hear how frustrating it is to make a hair appointment, arrange for a class, plan to hang out with friends, or try to work (and the last can be the worst because it involves a greater time commitment), and then, *bingo*, everything's off. It's like some kind of reverse magic. No sooner do you make plans and invest anticipation and emotion in them than that's the day your partner gets forced/mandatoried or sent out to a fire for fourteen days.

It can be downright devastating, depending on your firefighter to use their days off helping you, relieving you of some of the added weight you're bearing on your shoulders simply by being a significant other in the fire world. The good thing is that the devastation is preventable when you become more independent. And you do that by always having a backup plan. Why? So you are not the one who is constantly sacrificing. So your relationship won't dissolve in a pool of bitterness.

Here are just a few suggestions to help you start building a backup network, circle of support, and more independent life. If you have children, this is a necessity.

- Make friends with other fire service significant others, so you can take turns watching the kids.

- Find a neighborhood teenager you trust to babysit, that all the friends in your area can use.

- Keep the number of a professional babysitting or nanny service on hand. Yes, it costs more than your friend's teenage daughter, but it is well worth having a contact in case an emergency comes up.

- If you don't work, join daytime groups where you can meet other parents: art and cooking classes, book groups, scheduled Zumba, or other fitness courses.

I suggest making sure you have day care of some kind, one day at least, but preferably two days a week, so you can have time to yourself. If worse comes to worst, and you feel you need to escape from younger children before you tear your hair out, count your blessings if you live anywhere near an Ikea or other large retailer that has a fun place to park kids so they can have supervised play while you shop. You don't even need to shop there. Once your kids are happily playing in the ball pit or on the jungle gym, you can head for the coffee shop and have an hour of peace with a book or magazine.

When your children reach school age, it gets easier if you work at it. It isn't difficult to make friends with other parents through school activities or your kids' sports. Other parents are a dependable resource, if you ever need someone to pick up your offspring at, or drive them to, school. And, as I was, be prepared to help other parents out, too. This can never be a one-way street.

If you've been in a relationship for a long time, becoming independent again can be a challenge, but you need to rise to it. Endeavors such as hiking or joining a yoga class come with a bonus: they will relieve your tension and resentment. It's also good to make plans to do things on your own, from going to a museum exhibition or the ballet (trust me, no one thinks you're weird for being alone) to taking on a long-overdue project like painting the spare room.

Have a charity or outside interest that could use some volunteers? You will make new friends easily by getting involved, plus you will have the satisfaction of helping a cause you care about. Anything from volunteering at a charity shop to being a museum or visitor center docent will help, and you will meet women with and without children who, like you, might be looking to expand their circles of support.

In the backup plan department, don't relegate this solely to when you need someone's help with something. If your significant other is called in to work when you were planning, say, a drive to a nearby lake or an overnight in a scenic town, don't cancel until you see if someone else might want to accompany you.

It's become a joke, with my friends. Every year, Jeff and I take a trip in December. Well, the past few years have given us later-than-usual fire seasons. So, my friends are always calling or texting to let me know they are available if Jeff happens to be sent to a fire.

I am not saying you should exclude or stop depending on your firefighter. It's just extremely important for you and your relationship that you don't feel as if you are always the one to make sacrifices. It took me a while to accept that my husband wasn't picking fire over me, but that when they call, he has to go. So I always have a plan B if I need it.

Stepping Up and Owning Your Responsibility

As a long-time fire wife, I promise you that this life we have chosen has many rewards and adventures. Our firefighters have a passion and craving for adventure you won't see much of elsewhere. If you're new to this and nervous, stay positive! You will both love and hate the life, but as long as you take ownership of your happiness, you will have a good relationship and come to love the fire world itself.

This means that if you're not happy, you need to do something about it. Owning your responsibility is an active, not passive, state. What if you aren't sure what to do differently in order to make things better? Then it is your responsibility to reach out and get help. That doesn't always mean you need a counselor. There are books (like this one) that can help give you some ideas of what might work better. Another option could be a couples retreat or workshop. If these things don't work, then you can seek professional help.

Too often, by the time couples come to me, they have waited too long. Their relationship is in bad shape, totally stuck, seemingly at a dead end. This means I can't help some of them. That is a source of great sadness for me, but I'm being honest. When your relationship has been on life support, it can be too late to salvage it. That's why you need to seek help sooner rather than later.

At this point in my life and marriage, I think everyone would benefit from counseling once in a while. If that sounds too dramatic, ask yourself this: where else could you get help from someone with an objective perspective? Your family? Uh, no. Your friends? No way. These people can never be objective, no matter how hard they try— not to mention that they aren't trained to help you sort through your tangled emotions and competing complaints in a rational manner.

One of the great things about people is that they evolve. Humans facing change in their lives need to adapt. Both alone and together, everyone can use a little help at times. Change can be difficult for some, as can even the natural life stages we all go through (new job, new baby, move to another city, loss of a parent), but sometimes we also need help in adapting to our *partner*'s changes. Jeff and I have received counseling both individually and as a couple. It has always been positive—helping us see things in a different light, making us feel closer. Counseling is never about who's wrong and who's right. Disagreements and problems are rarely that cut and dried. Being emotionally entrenched in an argument or fraught situation makes it impossible to examine it from an unemotional perspective, and that's where an outside person coming in is a necessity. In a stalemate, no one comes out ahead.

I see this all the time when couples consult me. Maybe they start out finger-pointing, their pent-up emotions pouring out in a lot of he-says-this or she-does-that comments. Even if calm, they tend to be locked into their personal point of view, and since these points of view are conflicting, they get stuck and can't come up with solutions, no matter how they try. I can assure you that, having been in the same situation with Jeff, I know how hard you have probably tried, to no avail, because that's how hard we tried, over and over again. We needed a third voice.

Couples who come to me need a third voice, and that voice is mine. I can tell you that it works, not only because of the couples I've worked with, but because Jeff and I are still together and happy. Over the years, I've learned how to get out of my own stubborn way and be able to see Jeff's point of view (even though I might still feel I'm always right). Someone else can guide both of you into walking a mile in your partner's shoes. I won't tell you that you will wake up one day and your relationship or your life in general will be the greatest it could possibly be. But every step moves you forward. Life is a process and involves change. You have to live it with intention.

Owning your responsibility also means accepting that you need to be flexible. Flexibility and communication are the two most important skills in a fire relationship. That means almost everything will have to be a compromise, if you are to thrive. As for compromise, it means that sometimes you will bear the burden of family responsibility, and sometimes your partner will bear it instead.

Fifty-fifty. That's what we're always told relationships should be. But that's never true 100 percent of the time—and certainly not in fire families. Some days I may have to give 120 percent because Jeff is working or ill, or has something to take care of. The ratio can flip overnight and for any reason. When it flips against you, you need to remember you are on a team, and that, while everyone contributes, it is never perfectly equal. Not every player gets the MVP award, but everyone on the team is important.

It can be hard for us at times, but we have to be understanding and compassionate about our firefighters not always being able to engage as much as we would like. This does not relieve them of their responsibilities, one of which is taking care of themselves. They need to get enough rest, take time to decompress, and seek counseling if they need it—and not just for their own sake, but because they owe us the best version of themselves. Our responsibility is not to take things personally, not to internalize their disconnect.

Yes, if the disconnect goes on for an extended period, we need to call them out on it. We mustn't see ourselves as victims or behave as if we are. The important thing is to be nonjudgmental, because chances are, our firefighters don't realize they're letting us down. They don't even know how they feel.

The best approach is to call them out while keeping in mind that they probably believe they are doing the best they can. They are try-ing to push through as they have been taught to do. When we discuss communication skills and exercises, you will learn how to resolve these disconnects, not with fighting and bitterness but as team members.

Relax and Be More Flexible

In a relationship with a firefighter, you have no choice but to be flexible. You might not like it, but that's the way it is. One of the characteristics of flexibility is being bendable; that includes being loose with bending rules that might be rigidly adhered to in other families.

Take holidays, for instance. In our family, we rarely celebrate holidays on their actual days. My kids still ask me on what day we will be celebrating Christmas or Mother's Day. I always say, "It's Christmas when I tell you it is." Don't worry—this will not permanently damage your kids. They adapt much better than adults do.

To make up for our not being exactly like their friends' families, I created rituals for the kids when Jeff was working, so they wouldn't feel out of it but special and valued instead. One of our big things was camping out—in the living room. We would stock up with movies and fast food before settling in on the floor with our blankets and sleeping bags. It was always great fun. I confess that when Jeff wanted to do it with us, we told him he couldn't, that it was our special thing. It was, and the whole point of it was to make the kids not feel bad that their dad wasn't always there for them, at least not physically.

Another family ritual I tell my firefighter and significant others' classes about is that I let the kids take off a day from school when Jeff came home from a fourteen-day or longer assignment. I never kept them home on Day One, because firefighters need that time to decompress, but the next day or the day after is always good. You can plan something fun to do together or hang out at home.

The kids are overjoyed to be together as a family, with the added joy of playing hooky for a day. And no kid ever lost a scholarship opportunity by taking the occasional day off. This is what I mean by being flexible and adjusting. You just have to get into the habit of shifting your outlook a bit and creating a lifestyle that works with this job and its lifestyle demands.

Because they don't get to spend an ideal amount of time together, you can help make sure your kids keep in touch with your firefighter on workdays. When my kids were little, we didn't have FaceTime or Skype, and had to rely on phone calls. But these apps now make keeping your family in contact a no-brainer.

One of my friends has her firefighter husband call on FaceTime at dinner when he can. She puts the phone in the middle of the table, and the family dines together. Firefighters can also use these apps to read books to their children at bedtime. The key here is reducing separation anxiety for the kids, and keeping bonds strong between the adults. It also helped, when Kyle was a toddler, that Jeff would leave his work T-shirt that smelled like him at home with Kyle. Kyle called it his "dad shirp," and he carried it with him everyplace. When he was upset or just missing Jeff, he would rub it on his face and say, "I love my dad shirp."

For real-life face time, if you live close enough to the station, you can stop by with the kids and, when they get older, they can go on ride-outs with their firefighter parent. This is also a way to make sure the kids get to see Dad on at least some holidays. And as I said earlier, Jeff and I have our own daily phone call rituals, which keep us feeling close and connected.

What if your firefighter isn't as open or flexible as you are? Don't give up. Remember, firefighters are used to being in control of, and even consciously repressing, their emotions. When you attempt to do things differently, they might not be receptive to that. So it's up to you to keep plugging away at improving your firefighter's flexibility. We'll talk about that more in the next chapter, because one of the vital tools is a good channel of communication. For now, I will say it is wiser not to attempt to try to get your partner to change in the middle of a fight, or when they have just walked through the front door. Timing is everything! The exercises I'll provide will help with these conversations. And if you still don't make headway, it's an indication that you should consider a counselor.

If you're not sure what needs to be fixed, start keeping a list so that when you sit down to talk, alone together or with a counselor, you have concrete concerns. Simply saying, "I'm not happy," or, "I don't feel valued," gets you nowhere. It's easy to get locked into the routine of life and become unaware of what is bugging you to the point that you, as well as your firefighter, don't see the disconnect in your relationship or your family.

This might be an excellent time to plan a short getaway. When you change the scenery, you trick your brain into resetting and paying attention. Getting up and doing the same thing every day can result in our brains going into autopilot mode, so we're not as present as we need to be. You might be surprised at how many people reveal they have had sudden insights into their lives while doing nothing more than standing on a bridge looking at a river flow past, or driving along a country lane.

Now, you might be thinking, "Sure, I'd love to go away with my partner, but we can't afford it." Or, "We don't have time." Getting away doesn't mean flying away to Europe or Hawaii, as nice as that would be. Be creative and look around where you live. Jeff and I live twenty-five minutes away from a ski resort. We love to go skiing midweek when the crowds aren't there. In the spring and summer, those slopes become mountain bike and hiking trails, so we always have inexpensive options.

Quick getaways and short-term planning are necessary much of the time for fire families, but you needn't get locked into that, either. If you want to go away for a couple of days, and your partner can't go along, having those backups in place means you will be able to find a friend who would love to go.

When you do go on an "away" holiday with your significant other, enjoy yourself, but don't expect your firefighter to jump right in immediately.

Here's an example of what I mean. I was eager for a relaxing beach vacation, so I convinced Jeff we should go to a Jamaican resort. Of course, being a regimented firefighter, he asked, even before agreeing to the trip, "What would we do there?"

You would think I had asked him to come camping in the middle of the Sahara! I described what I envisioned: reclining on lounges close to the water's edge, swimming in the Caribbean, drinking the kind of exotic cocktails that come in big glasses with tiny paper umbrellas and fruit trimmings. I could see he wasn't quite taking that in—to a task-oriented firefighter, it all translates as doing *nothing*—but he said, sure, let's do it.

When we got there, he turned into my reluctant date. If you have traveled with your firefighter, I know you've been there, even if it wasn't Jamaica.

On the first day, as we stretched out on our lounge chairs, slathered in sunscreen and sipping our drinks, I was initially in heaven, but I could feel that Jeff was twitchy and restless. The urge to be doing something specific, a duty, was so ingrained that he wasn't having an easy time. So now, I'm anxious, too.

At first, I kept trying to think of something we could get up and do—until I realized I didn't want to do anything but what I had already told him were my priorities: lying there and relaxing. *I'm not giving in. I'm not giving in,* I chanted silently, *I'm not moving from this lounge.* And you know what happened? Jeff made friends, and he started playing beach volleyball twice a day. That's how he knew what time it was. He played beach volleyball at eleven and four, eleven and four, every day. Now he had a routine! It was awesome.

Meanwhile, I stretched out on the beach, and then I went scuba diving, because they had free group dives, and Jeff doesn't dive. I would go out scuba diving for hours. When I'd come back in and see him playing volleyball and hanging with new friends, I was at peace. I knew he had struggled, because he wanted regimentation. He had concerns. *What are we going to do today? What's the agenda today?* And it was hard for him to accept that we didn't have one. But as soon as he managed to go with the flow, he had a great time and got the relaxation and escape he needed.

If you are thinking, *Wow. Not my firefighter,* you are lucky. Everything in this book isn't an absolute for everyone. Some firefighters don't struggle with relaxing away from work. But a majority of them do. Watching my husband finally turn off his work brain and enjoy being my husband always warms my heart and reminds me it's all worth it. It's enough to get me through another fire season. Our vacations or getaways bring out the Jeff I married.

How do you start to change if you haven't been flexible, haven't been owning your responsibility? You start right here. Before you go on to the next chapter, spend some time and make your list. What would you change in your relationship if you could? Try to not make this list a rap sheet of all the things you have stored up in your head. This is an opportunity to write down what you want to change in your relationship, like, "I want to go out more with my partner," or, "I want to feel heard," or, "I need more help with chores or parenting."

How many people are in your circle of trust? Do you have a list of volunteer helpers when you need a hand with the kids or chores? Do you have another list of paid helpers for when friends are tied up? Who do you have to hang out with? If you don't know enough people, what would you consider doing to meet more? What activities could you do, even when alone, to make yourself feel less lonely? What have you always wanted to do yet always put off that you might have time for now?

If you have kids, you can add them to your list, too. What activities could you do with your children that would get all of you out of the house? What places in your town will responsibly care for your kids for free while you shop or have a coffee? What are some day trips you can take, with or without the kids? What overnight trips would you like to do, with and without the kids, with and without your partner, alone or with a friend?

When you have all your lists together, you are almost ready to talk to your firefighter about how you would like to shake things up a little bit and where you will need some help. But before you do, read the next chapter, because I'm sure it will make the process of communicating all this much easier for both of you.

CHAPTER SEVEN
Talk Isn't Cheap Unless You Make It that Way

HAVE I STRESSED COMMUNICATION ENOUGH? I know I haven't stressed it too much, because that is impossible. You might speak to your firefighter every day, but that doesn't mean you're truly communicating—that you are sharing your worries and concerns. There is no more important area of practice, in terms of keeping your marriage strong and preventing divorce, than acquiring dependable communication skills.

I know it often seems easier to avoid dealing with any of this than to confront it. I say this as someone who spent the first years of my marriage tiptoeing around my husband most of the time, only to blow up and start fights out of resentment when I was feeling fed up. I learned the hard way, which means I learned after being sure more than once that we weren't going to make it. I want you to succeed and build a stronger marriage as we did. Good communication skills with good listening skills are the golden keys to that.

Let's talk about how you start. You don't do this by blurting out, "We have to talk!" as soon as your firefighter comes through the door. Or announcing it in front of anyone else. And you *never* start in the middle of an ongoing argument.

The best way to have what might be the most important conversation in your marriage is to get your partner on the team by saying you would like to try to resolve some of the issues you think are a problem for both of you in your relationship. Say you would like to set time aside to do that. You can make a date for a time when the kids, if you have a family, won't be home. It's helpful to many couples to make lists of the issues they feel are most important—not necessarily to go through the list item by item, but to get your feelings on paper so you know what you want to say.

Keep in mind that you may not be able to resolve everything in a single conversation, or even several, especially if you have both become locked into the conflicts. You should be prepared to calmly explain the most important challenges you think you are facing as a couple. You need to face your firefighter having mutually agreed to stay calm, and not get defensive or start making excuses about your behavior. You won't be in a court of law or a competition, nor are you asking for a favor. You are planning to work together as a team. And keep in mind that if either of you makes anything into a battle, it will end up going in circles and getting nothing accomplished. Remember, losing is not in a firefighter's nature.

First, there are some general rules that will help you in reaching a resolution and a satisfying outcome:

1. Listen closely. What you will be hearing is as important as what you will say.

2. Work at it. Respect the fact that, whether or not you agree with what your partner is saying, they are stating their truth, what is true to them and what they feel.

3. Concentrate on keeping your body language positive and open. You don't need to be smiling widely, but you should be looking alert and interested rather than bored or sullen or rolling your eyes.

4. Don't interrupt or shout. That can turn the conversation into yet another argument.

5. Try to celebrate the issues you agree on and show your appreciation when you can.

6. Be confident and don't rush—think before speaking, ask for clarification if you don't understand.

7. Stick to the topic at hand. Don't go off on tangents. Stay within the parameters of any topic you are on. For instance, if you want to bring out how it troubles you that your firefighter wants to stay home all the time on days off, rather than go out with other couples, don't suddenly interject something about their not being willing to pick up the kids at school or stop at the supermarket.

Conquering the Four Horsemen

Dr. John Gottman, of the Gottman Institute, has been named one of the "Top 10 Most Influential Therapists" of the past quarter century by the Psychotherapy Networker, and he is a leader in the field of couples therapy. What he calls the "Four Horsemen" are the four characteristics of poor communication for couples. They are defensiveness, criticism, contempt, and stonewalling. Let's go through them one by one, and I'll explain what they mean to me.

Defensiveness—Anytime you respond to your partner's complaint or statement with "But you..." or, "I wouldn't do that if you didn't..." or any other type of negative statement like this. These statements are attempts to relieve you of responsibility and place the blame solely with your partner. It is not only a more aggressive way of playing the victim, it slams the door on resolution. If you blame others, make excuses for yourself, or always answer a complaint with another one, grow up. You're too old to play "But they started it!" This is something children do.

This horseman was the most prominent one in my house. If I asked Jeff, "Is something wrong?" he would respond, "No, I'm just tired. I worked all night. Sorry." That "Sorry" was said with sarcasm as if I had no clue what being tired felt like because, no, my kids weren't up all night.

Criticism—This is another blaming mechanism, characterized by hurling generalized charges that don't criticize an action or specific event, but the other person's entire being. When you say "you never..." or "you always..." it is only natural for your partner to get defensive and say, "C'mon, it's you who always..." or "When was the last time you...." Generalizing also applies to tossing out personal labels on the order of "You're selfish!" or "You're a nag!" Remember, this is not about scoring points. This is a team-building exercise. You can criticize the behavior without attacking the person.

I am probably guilty of this one. I felt so overwhelmed with the kids and him being gone all the time that I tended to blame Jeff for it. Even if he wasn't that grumpy, I would say, "You're always tired and never want to hang out or do anything." Of course, this wasn't completely true, because he would often do things with us and have fun.

Contempt—Mocking, scorning, or demeaning your partner in any way, whether with words, tone of voice (sarcasm), or making faces (sneering) is pretty much like hitchhiking to divorce court. Words said in anger that belittle another person are not easily forgotten. They alone can break up a marriage.

What if your partner aims contempt your way? The best way to handle it is to stay calm. Say, "Don't just tell me I'm stupid/silly/wrong. Explain why you feel that way so I can understand." Don't even try to disguise your contempt by being condescending.

This one is a slippery slope for fire families, because one of the main ways we communicate is through jokes and sarcasm. Where this becomes negative is if, during a fight, you capitalize on sensitive information about the other person, making a joke or being condescending.

Stonewalling—This is most typically a man's behavior, rather than a woman's, but both sexes can stonewall when they don't want to deal with something. It is threatening to most of us to bare our souls about things that deeply affect us in intimate relationships. Some people will stonewall when they feel overwhelmed. Rather than cry or express their hurt or bewilderment, they will shut down. Both of you should agree to taking occasional breaks during your discussions—perhaps either of you raising a hand as a signal for a timeout to collect yourselves. But, as with international diplomacy, you need to come back to the table. Withdrawing is not a solution for conflict. It is impossible to resolve a two-person conflict if one of the parties refuses to talk. Never forget: pots on simmer boil over just as those bubbling away furiously do.

Communications Keys

How can you make your way through this communication minefield and come out safely on the other side? First, you can make sure always to treat your partner and their complaints or problems with respect. Second, you should make sure some requests or complaints are off-limits.

A big complaint or request I hear often in therapy is about the amount of sex or lack of sex in the relationship. Sex is an important element to an intimate relationship; however, it can't be the most important thing. Your relationship must be able to stand alone without sex.

Often, sex is used as a weapon. Sometimes the man will say, "I do all these things for you, and buy you stuff, the least you can do is give me sex." This is a no-no—because it basically implies you think you're paying for your sex. It can make your partner feel less valued.

Women, too, can be bad about withholding sex as a punishment. Both examples will tear a relationship down faster than anything else. It's okay to talk about sexual problems, but you should try to broach subjects without finger-pointing, by treating anything that comes up as "our problem" rather than "your problem."

Phrasing your complaints in a blame-free manner will make your partner more willing to listen without calling in any of the Four Horsemen to turn your relationship into an apocalypse. Here's a fill-in-the-blanks phrase I think you'll find helpful: "I feel _____ when you _____ because _____ I need _____." I'll be explaining this vital tool more in-depth in just a bit.

Think positive! Start by phrasing things positively. Rather than saying, "We never go anywhere anymore. I don't want staycations," start your criticism on a positive note. For example, you could say something like, "I always loved when we would drive up to the lake and stay at that beautiful lodge for the weekend. Remember? I want us to take trips like that again, and not stay home all the time." Any sentence you start with "I" means you're taking ownership of your feelings and not making the other person responsible. One favorite I hear all the time is, "You make me so angry." Uh-uh. You're in control of your own emotions. Breaking down what is bothering you with the "I feel" statements will be more effective and decrease the urge to be defensive.

Always take responsibility for your own faults. Apologize, even if the complaint doesn't strike you as especially serious. You won't spontaneously combust if you say something on the order of, "I'm genuinely sorry it I threw away all of last week's junk mail. I honestly didn't realize you liked going through it." But you can feel free to add, "Let's just put a special box for it in the family room, so it isn't all over the house."

Work on making mutual commitments to change and standing by them. If you promise to make pot roast on your partner's first night home after their shift for the rest of the year, do it. Otherwise, seek a compromise. In love as well as business or government, compromises go both ways. They are the key to negotiation and diplomacy.

Work Together to Work Things Out

You can cement your partnership by working together to become better at expressing your needs. I do couples workshops for firefighters and their significant others to help them in becoming more open about stating and resolving problems.

In this section, I'm going to tell you about some exercises you and your firefighter can work on to communicate more openly and honestly yet without ending up in an argument.

ACTIVITY ONE: *"I Feel" Statements*

I'd like to talk a bit more about generalizations, and why it is important to work on not starting statements with "you never" or "you always." Think about it for a minute and ask yourself, *How do I feel when someone starts out a sentence accusing me of something?* The natural reaction is to go on the defense, wanting to explain or defend your actions. This never goes anywhere healthy or leads to resolving a conflict. What ends up happening is another argument, with both parties walking away angry about yet another issue.

When a couple comes into my office, the first exercise I have them do is work on "I feel" statements, which consist of four sentences about how you feel. It's about taking ownership of your own feelings, rather than telling your partner what they did wrong. This goes with another issue I often see, which is that one of the parties says too much before getting to the point or saying how they feel. When someone does this, it feels like a lecture or being talked *at*—either of which makes the other partner shut down and stop listening. This was one of the biggest issues Jeff and I had to work on. I felt like Jeff was defensive when I brought up anything, which caused me to: 1. stop talking to him about issues and hold them in, 2. build up resentments toward him, and 3. feel unsafe opening up to him about anything. Naturally, this created distance in our relationship.

This activity works because it forges a clear and simple path to more open conversations. When you approach each other this way, neither of you can argue about how the other person feels, or defend why you act a certain way. We are all allowed to have feelings about situations without judgments. Feelings aren't right or wrong—they just are. So, when you try this out, make a conscious effort to be quiet, listen, and say "Okay." This takes practice. But anything worth having is worth the practice and effort you need to put into it.

So let me explain how it works. In each of the examples below, the underlined part should be filled in with what you wish to express. The *Appendix* has forms for you to work with, to put your thoughts in order.

- *I feel* <u>hurt</u>. - You insert one feeling word, just one. Many people have tried to stick in "I feel that you always" here, because that's been their way of communication. All you get to put here is one feeling word.

- *When you* <u>come home and notice the one thing I didn't do</u>. - Again, you mustn't let the word "always" sneak in here. Just insert the behavior that you're feeling something about. Make sure it's just one behavior, like slamming doors, not playing with the kids, or ignoring you when you ask about the day.

- *Because* it makes me feel like what I do isn't good enough for you. - This is your free spot to let your partner know how their behavior affects you. Be careful not to be nasty, sarcastic, or accusing. Keep the focus on you and how you feel.

- *I need you* to notice the things I did do more than what I didn't. This sentence is where you will state your needs, and what you are asking for from the other person, in order to feel better about the situation. Beware, because this is where it can go wrong. If you are the listener, the urge can be strong to argue or say, "Well, you do this!" or get defensive. Again, bite your tongue, listen, and hear what is being said. What makes a good relationship is the two of you having your own thoughts and ideas. It would be boring if you thought the same things. It's okay for us to have different beliefs without being offended.

ACTIVITY TWO: *Getting to Know Each Other and How Well You Communicate*

There are two separate activities that require you to interview each other. You may be thinking, *That's stupid. I know my partner well.* True though that may be, the longer we are together, the more we change. It is good to always be intentional about keeping in touch with how your partner has evolved. Trust me, you will learn things you didn't know before. Most people don't really listen well, because they start thinking of what they're going to say next. This causes them to miss some of the content of the conversation. This activity is meant for you to get to know each other better and practice your active listening skills. If you get defensive or start arguing, your partner will shut down.

These are some rules that will help you:

1. Take turns asking each other the questions on the sheet you can copy from the *Appendix*.

2. Write down what your partner says. This allows you to hear exactly what they are saying without misinterpreting their statements.

3. Read the answer back to make sure you got it right.

4. You can ask one clarifying question as you do this, but neither party is allowed to argue or make their partner prove themselves.

5. Once all the questions have been answered, switch and let your partner ask the questions. The same rules apply.

ACTIVITY THREE: *How Do We Talk about Your Job?*

I understand not everyone has trouble talking about what their firefighter does and sees. However, I have heard many firefighters and their significant others say they're not sure what to ask or say or whether they should give their partner space. This can be a tricky conversation, for some.

Some firefighters have shared that they don't want to burden their significant others with the bad things they see. But there is a big drawback to this behavior. Your firefighter loves what they do, and they are passionate about the job and their crews. If we don't talk about it at all, or very little, we are missing out on a major part of our firefighter's heart and soul. Every couple is different, so you have to find what works for your relationship. For Jeff and me, it was somewhat easy, since I had worked in EMS and seen some really bad calls myself. Jeff and I have always talked about his calls, gross stuff and all. This may not work for you, so you have to set the boundaries. Maybe ask your firefighter if—when they get called to a bad car crash, for example— they would please leave out the details when they talk to you.

I'm not telling you how to set this up or what is right or wrong. All I am saying is that the conversation has to happen. It will draw you closer if you both feel connected when it comes to the world of firefighting.

There is an opposite pole to oversharing details, and that is silent suffering. As much as firefighters love black humor, and can make jokes about terrible things, that is as much a defense mechanism as a dark sense of humor. Some days are good, some are bad, and some are very bad. If your firefighter comes home in a silent and somber mood, you can try asking about funny calls they might have had that day, as sometimes that will take them out of whatever their thoughts have been dwelling on.

If that doesn't work, they might genuinely need time to sort it all out on their own, in which case you can't go wrong by telling them, "I'm here if you want to talk." This signals that you understand something bad has gone on as well as that you are there to listen if they want.

The more you comprehend the job, of course, the more you can read the signals and experience personally what your firefighter's work life is about. If you haven't done any ride-outs, now is the time to start.

ACTIVITY FOUR: *Gratitude*

It's easy to get caught up in our daily lives and lose track of how much we do for each other. It's not that we don't appreciate each other— we just forget to say it out loud. Even when I was speaking to 350 firefighters at the Montecito mudslides about signs and symptoms of stress and PTSD, I reminded them that while their work is very hard, their partners' role—waiting for them to come home, hoping they are all right, worrying endlessly—is also hard. It's different, but just as hard. Letting each other know how much you appreciate having them in your life is not an expensive gift, but it is worth more than any money in the world. And that applies to both of you.

Complete the sentences on the list of gratitude in the *Appendix* and read them to each other.

ACTIVITY FIVE: *Family Rules*

Frequently, in a fire family, there is some chaos due to the different environments the kids have to adapt to. Add your different parenting styles, and this can be another source of conflict. Creating family rules with prearranged consequences in place gives some structure and consistency for both kids and parents. Plus, creating those rules is an excellent way of getting to know your kids and their priorities better.

Sit together as a family and come up with no more than five family rules that everyone, adults included, will follow. Allow kids to give input at all stages. Allowing them to be and feel part of the process will make them more willing to follow the rules.

Whenever possible, these rules should be addressed in terms of what you want rather than don't want. Examples might include "Be respectful to each other," or, "Chores will be completed before privileges are granted." And, again, everyone in the family must agree to the rules, including things like "No cussing" or "No name-calling" (in these cases, stating what you don't want is okay and simpler). Be sure and discuss as a family what each rule means in terms of your family. It is important that everyone understand and agree upon the rules.

Create consequences for rules being broken. Ask your kids what they think is a good consequence for each rule, making this a discussion rather than an opportunity for scolding or defensive behavior. Don't position the consequences as "punishments," but simply as the price to be paid for breaking the rule. Once a fair consequence for each rule has been agreed on, write it on the same paper or board opposite its rule. Make it clear that all of you decided the rules and they must never be treated as a joke.

When a rule is broken, you can merely refer to the family rules and remind your kids (or your cussing partner!) that they discussed and agreed to these.

Put the final copy of the family rules with the consequences on it in a visible area of the house so everyone can be reminded of them daily.

Work Together to Show Your Love

Life for a fire couple or family is complicated. It is busy and hectic. It's easy, too easy at times, to forget to make an effort to show affection. But it can be done, if you work at it, and it will make the complications and busyness less stressful.

A 1995 book by Baptist pastor Gary Chapman called *The Five Love Languages: How to Express Heartfelt Commitment to Your Mate* points out how important it is to show your feelings and gratitude. The five languages are quality time and the sharing and giving of it; gifts, whether large or small; words of affirmation, to remind your partner how much you appreciate them; physical touch; and acts of service or devotion.

According to Chapman, each person has one primary and one secondary love language. In other words, you might not show your love in the same manner your firefighter does. You might be into giving gifts and quality time, while your partner is more of a physical touch and devotion sort of person. You mustn't expect your significant other to act as you do; you just need to accept and appreciate their expressions of love and be mindful of expressing your own love in return.

If nothing seems to work for you—if you think you have communicated as best you can, and you have worked together to resolve your difficulties, to no avail—that is a signal that you should discuss going for counseling.

What if your partner refuses to go? Go on your own. If you seek counseling as a couple, make it a date day, even if it means bringing in a babysitter. After all, you are taking a step in the right direction, which is something to celebrate.

EPILOGUE
Good to Go

LESS THAN A YEAR AGO, I started writing this book. A lot has happened since then. My son Kyle graduated the fire academy and will start his seasonal firefighter position. He also was accepted to a paramedic program.

My daughter Megan got engaged and recently started working in youth probation. I started my own private counseling practice. My husband Jeff and I took a romantic European river cruise for our twenty-first wedding anniversary. You can tell we're a fire couple, because we went in December, when our actual anniversary is in August. This isn't a normal season when others would choose that type of vacation, but it is the ideal time to take a break from the fire world; it used to be more ideal, because fire season was over by November, but these last couple of years, it has gone into December. Our trip was a fantastic, romantic, and relaxing adventure through a winter wonderland, and we loved every minute of it. And, yes, in the past year, I also finished this book.

I'm telling you this for an important reason: to show how much change can take place in a single year and how much life holds for you. I told you at the beginning my four reasons for writing about the world we share, and I think and hope I have fulfilled my promise to you.

The first reason was to assure you that you're not alone. Your thoughts and feelings as part of the fire world are, I know, not just from my experiences but from the lives of others I have counseled, unique unto you and yet remarkably similar to what the rest of us go through. I hope you have laughed at some of the similarities and that others have made both you and your partner more aware of what the other is going through.

I was recently talking to firefighters at a California fire department about peer support, and I brought up the subject of work brain versus home brain. The chief there later told me that my words were literally life-changing. He said he'd always known that "something" was going on with him, but he had never found the words for it. After he heard me explain the concept, it resonated deeply. He went home, gathered his wife and children around him, and said, "I'm sorry I've been a jerk for the last twenty years, but I understand why, now."

He explained he had never understood that what he did and felt had some logic behind it or a rationale. His wife told me they had all cried together, and she said, "He has literally been a different man."

It's like Maya Angelou said: "When you know better, you do better."

Realizations and the commitment to change can come suddenly once you "get it" and everything falls into place. But it's okay if you and your partner need a little more time. We all grow and learn at a different pace.

I also told you that being married, engaged, or committed to anyone in the fire service is a unique set of circumstances, and that I would help you fully understand how and why. No marriage is perfect, and fire marriages aren't all minefields. But we have a different set of rules. My hope is that, with this book, I've been able to lay out some of those rules so you now have the words for what you are dealing with and know how to respond. I hope my personal story has helped you see that anyone can start out as oblivious as I was when I met Jeff, yet change and grow by working at it—and that until you're in it, you can't really imagine what a fire relationship is like. You have to fill your toolbox with new skills all the time. I hope I have equipped you with those so you can start immediately to make your relationship what you want it to be.

The third important principle I had to share is that you need to approach your relationship with the right mind-set and with expectations that are attainable and pertinent to your relationship. Your solutions will always be individual, based on the career and who you are.

This is not a cookie-cutter process. You will need to put in some work and compromise in order to get value out of it. It will be worth it. The activities laid out for you will help with that, and you can photocopy the pages in the appendices to fill out and organize your thoughts and actions.

This doesn't mean your marriage is in trouble. We should always be motivated to grow individually and as a couple. This takes constant practice and attention.

The keyword for the right mind-set is, and always will be, "compromise." That means no more finger-pointing and no using communication to punish your partner. No shouldering the blame or not making yourself heard in order to smooth things over, either. The tools in your toolbox are there to be used, but they must never be used as weapons in an attempt to act victimized or cast blame.

And, last, a firefighter relationship will grow and prosper only when it is an equal partnership. In a strong relationship, there is always something new and interesting to learn about the person with whom you share your life. What's been really rewarding for Jeff and me—and our kids, too—is that as we have written our parts and read each other's, we have grown in understanding where the other person was coming from. There were things Jeff wrote that I had never known about; I hadn't understood how he felt. There were parts that brought me to tears because I had no clue. This past year has been filled with ups and downs, but writing this book has helped us empathize with each other and brought the walls down a little further.

Throughout this book, I've wanted you to hear my husband's voice as well as mine. After all, we're a team, and I think his viewpoint will help you in grasping what your firefighter thinks and feels.

Here's what Jeff had to say about reaching this point: "It's almost surreal to think that this book is done. Mynda resisted for quite a while, but once she started, there was no stopping her. I saw the spark in her that attracted me from the moment we met. She was on a mission: a mission to help every fire couple out there; to help spread the word that you aren't in this alone; and that what you experience is pretty much the same for every fire couple. In the process, we sat and talked more often and openly. We learned a little bit more about each other every time. We relived some of our highs and lows, opened up on how we dealt with things, and all of a sudden it seemed that this book could go on forever. Through it all, we continued to have 'normal' family occurrences along with our fire family occurrences. Putting the thoughts together to spread the word didn't seem as difficult for Mynda and me as I thought it could be. While writing the book, she also introduced and began presenting a couples workshop she had developed. The problem areas were common; the fights were over common issues; the complaints, likewise, covered common issues. The validation of those commonalities for all of us needs to be recognized for what it is. Fire couple issues are common to all of us."

Putting everything into words in these pages has made me more certain of one thing than ever: whether it was you or your firefighter, or both of you, who didn't know any better, didn't grasp what was going on, now that you *do* know, *it's on you.* You need to live with intention and work together to build your life.

A quote from author Mindy Hale is worth keeping as your mantra. It's simple yet profound: "Happiness is letting go of what you think your life is supposed to look like and celebrating it for everything that it is."

I am celebrating everything my own life is with this book, my work, my family, and my website www.fullyinvolvedlife.com. I created the website as one more way to reassure you that you are not alone. I think you'll find it helpful in reminding you of that, as it's filled with resources and articles, plus a regular newsletter.

As for Jeff and me, we continue to celebrate our marriage and our careers every day. Since Jeff now insists he won't be retiring until I do, I can guarantee that we'll be sticking around the fire world for a long time.

And we must all celebrate that world. We are so lucky to be part of this amazing universe of heroes and hard work, dark humor and deep caring. We aren't like other couples, other families, any more than you and I are like significant others outside this world. I hope now that you have read this book, you, like me, will live with the certainty that you wouldn't change your life for anyone else's. We are truly "fully involved."

APPENDIX

Communication Activity Forms

Here are four forms you can photocopy. You and your firefighter can use these communicating more openly with each other. Check *Chapter Seven* to learn exactly how to fill these out.

ACTIVITY ONE: *Talking about How You Feel*

- *I feel* _____

  Insert one feeling word, just one.

- *When you* _____ .

  Insert the behavior that you're feeling something about.

- *Because* _____

  Let your partner know how their behavior affects you. Be careful not to be nasty, sarcastic, or accusing. Keep the focus on you and how you feel.

- *I need you to* _____

  State what you are asking for from the other person in order to feel better about the situation.

ACTIVITY TWO: *How Does Your Partner Feel?*

Take turns asking each other these questions.

1. Is it easy or difficult for you to admit to having weaknesses?

2. Do you feel like you can be yourself with me?

3. Does it feel safe to be vulnerable with me?

4. Do you feel like I love and accept you unconditionally?

5. Do you feel that I notice more of what you do right than what you do wrong?

6. Is it easy to approach me about the things you don't like about my behavior?

7. If the things that bother you about me never change will you still be okay with me?

8. Do you feel that I am as accepting of you now as I was early in our relationship?

9. Is there anything that I can do to improve the feelings of acceptance in our relationship?

ACTIVITY THREE: *Interviewing*

Take turns asking each other these questions. Do not argue or defend yourself, just listen. You may ask a follow-up question if you're unclear about the answer. Write your answers down.

1. Do you ever feel like I am argumentative regardless of what you bring up?

2. Do I ever change the subject or make a joke when you're talking to me?

3. When we are arguing, do I bring up the past instead of focusing on the present?

4. Does it seem like I always have to be right?

5. Do I ever jump in and give you advice when you are talking?

6. Do I ever misinterpret what you are saying and insist you mean something else?

7. Do you ever feel like I'm judging you when you speak?

ACTIVITY FOUR: *Talking About the Job*

Firefighter

- Do you worry about me while I'm at work?

- Do you ever want to know more about what I do or about my career?

- Do you want to know about my calls, and in how much detail?

- What don't you want to hear about?

Significant other

- Do you mind if I ask about your calls or how your shift went?

- Do you worry about burdening me?

- Do you want me to ask about your shift or would you rather tell me when you are ready?

- Does it bother you that there are some areas I prefer not to know too much about?

Gratitude List

I appreciate it when you _____

I am grateful for you because _____

I like the way you _____

I feel special when you _____

I am grateful for our relationship because _____

_____ makes our relationship special and unique.

_____ is one of your strengths.

I feel closest to you when _____

Thank you for _____

ACTIVITY SIX: *Four Steps to Apologizing*

1. Acknowledge the offending behavior. It's important that you express understanding and ownership of what you did that was hurtful. Example: "I didn't show up for our dinner date." Use "I" statements, saying, "I'm sorry that you were upset when I..."

2. State how the behavior was hurtful, and express remorse. This is an opportunity to put yourself in the other person's shoes and show empathy for his or her hurt and suffering. "This was thoughtless of me and caused you to worry and feel disrespected. I'm sorry." The explanation of extenuating circumstances could possibly come later—however, don't lead with this. It diminishes the impact of your apology, and appears to deflect responsibility from you to an external cause. Be authentic and humble, and don't apologize with an ulterior motive. Don't follow an apology with an accusation of how the other person's behavior contributed to this or another problem in your relationship. Doing so would be using your apology as leverage, and would be seen as less than genuine.

3. Make amends. Amendments mean changes in behavior. Tell the person what you'll do to make things right. Sometimes what have been harmed are feelings, rather than something tangible (such as a dented car that can be repaired).

4. Promise that the behavior won't happen again. True apologies go beyond words, and actions speak louder than they do. If you say sorry too many times without changing the behavior, it can take away the value of your apology. How can you ensure that the

offense won't be repeated? In the above example, you could be realistic and simply promise not to make ambitious promises you might not be able to keep. Make sure to follow through on your promise, so the other person doesn't question your trustworthiness and commitment to change.

Tips:

1. Write out your apology and role-play it with a friend, with a colleague, or in the mirror (I know it sounds silly, but it will help). However, don't rehearse your amends to the point where it sounds scripted. Be genuine when you apologize.

2. Apologize as soon as possible.

3. Let go of being "right"; the important thing is to show that you understand the other person's feelings, even if the two of you don't agree. It's okay to agree to disagree. Feelings aren't right or wrong—they just are.

4. Don't be vague about the offense; don't just say something like, "I'm sorry I was such a jerk."

5. Don't over-apologize and call yourself a terrible person, the scum of the earth, or a loser. Don't say such things as "I don't know why anyone would give me the time of day." This turns an apology into a pity party, and makes the conversation about you rather than making amends to the other person.

6. Don't expect instant forgiveness. Give the person time to heal. Don't impose a timetable on the other person's process. You

might say, "I know you may want some time to think about our conversation. I just wanted to tell you how sorry I am. I realize that it may take some time for me to demonstrate to you that I'm committed to changing my behavior."

7. Finally, offer yourself forgiveness. By apologizing, you've shown that you have recognized your transgression, demonstrated humility, and made amends where you can. You show that you intend to behave with integrity in the future. Now, let go of self-condemnation and move forward in love and compassion for both the other person and yourself.

How to Ruin an Apology

The following statements indicate a failure to accept responsibility for one's actions or words. If your statement is in any way self-serving, it is not an apology. You must avoid these when making the perfect apology.

1. Avoid "I'm sorry, but..." This is not an apology, but an attempt to shift blame away from yourself.

2. Avoid "I *want to* apologize..." This phrase is similar to saying, "I want to lose weight," but not going on a diet. It comes across as insincere to the listener.

3. Avoid "I'm sorry you felt that way..." This is quite insulting to the person who has been hurt.

4. Avoid "I'm sorry it happened." "It happened" is simply another way to resist taking responsibility for your own actions, words, or attitudes.

5. Avoid "I'm sorry *if* I hurt you." This statement suggests you have not realized the pain you have caused, and will likely insult the offended one.

6. Avoid groveling. State your apology simply and then be quiet and listen to the response.

7. Avoid blaming the other person for being hurt. This indicates a lack of sincerity and undermines the purpose of an apology.

8. Avoid lecturing to defend or explain your actions. Using too many words can become self-serving and can further damage the relationship.

Apology Checklist

Does your apology express...

- ☑ regret?
- ☑ understanding of the problem?
- ☑ understanding of the other's feelings?
- ☑ acceptance of responsibility?
- ☑ willingness to improve?

How to Find the Right Clinician:
Questions for Firefighters to Ask

Finding the right clinician can be difficult that understands what you do for a living can be difficult but not impossible. First responders can't just pull up the yellow pages and pick any clinician. For a firefighter to feel comfortable they need to feel like the clinician they are talking to gets it. You don't want to have to explain your job or find that the clinician is horrified by your stories. It is suggested that you interview the clinician on phone prior to seeing them. Below are some questions you can ask that will help you to determine if they are appropriate.

1. **Do you have experience working with firefighter, police or military populations? If so, how long have you worked with them?**

    It is a bonus if they have worked with first responders or military but not a must. The most important thing is their personality and willingness to learn.

2. **Would you be willing to participate in learning more about the fire culture by riding out or station visits?**

    Again, not a must to have previous experience but if you have personal knowledge or experience with a clinician that you believe has the right personality to work with firefighters than be open to teaching them.

3. **What is your experience working directly with PTSD, depression, anxiety and drug and alcohol issues? What treatment interventions do you use? Are you trained in EMDR? Do you give homework assignments?**

The traditional talk therapy does work well, however when working with PTSD for first responder's alternative treatment is necessary. Treatments that have been proven to be effective in short-term therapy are, CBT, DBT, and EMDR. Also, a clinician who uses homework between sessions is also demonstrating a skill of using most of the session time as well as holding the client accountable for his/her own recovery.

4. **Do you offer appointments within 3 days or an on-call clinician?**

If you or a co-worker are in crisis finding a clinician to talk to right away is critical. However, if they don't have any appointments right away you can go to any emergency room to get help. Don't wait or say. "forget it" because it doesn't work out right away. You can also always call the national suicide hotline 24 hours a day: **1-800-273-8255**.

5. **Do you prescribe medication? If not, do you work closely with a doctor that does?**

Being able to prescribe medication isn't a must. Most clinicians don't but they need to know where to refer you if that is something needed.

MYNDA OHS is a recognized expert and speaker on firefighter wellness issues, with over fourteen years' experience in crisis intervention and suicide prevention. A former EMT whose life changed when she married a firefighter, who is now a Southern California battalion chief, she went back to school and garnered two master's degrees followed by a PhD in family studies from Loma Linda University. She has provided care and counseling in the aftermath of numerous line of duty deaths, the San Bernardino terrorist attack, the Las Vegas massacre, the Montecito mudslides, and many on-site critical incident situations. A licensed marriage and family therapist, Mynda has her own practice, which includes fire world couples counseling.

MORE INFORMATION
can be found on her website
www.fullyinvolvedlife.com

Made in the USA
Middletown, DE
11 April 2022

64002973R00106